THE EMOTIONS BEHIND BULLYING BEHAVIOUR

Your simple guide to Emotional Freedom Techniques – Tapping!

TAP OUT NEGATIVITY AND TAP INTO YOUR HAPPINESS

By

Sue Suchocki
Applied Techniques Training

www.appliedtechniques.net
Bonus – Online Tapping Group Invitation
facebook.com/groups/bullyingbehaviour/

This book is dedicated to the person who is the target of bullying behaviour or has been hurt by bullying, and the person who identifies as the perpetrator of bullying behaviours or the bully, and for those who support them, with the hope that each person can find inner peace through understanding and the use of Emotional Freedom Techniques - Tapping!

My love and thanks go to my husband, children, granddaughter and siblings for their support. A special thanks to two amazing ladies, one who introduced me to Emotional Freedom Techniques in 2008, Pamela O'Leary - Guided Solutions, and my mentor Dr Peta Stapleton.

My thanks also to Kenneth Nathan for sharing his knowledge of bullying behaviours through
"Managing The Bull".

Finally, to the women who inspire me - my Mother, my daughter, Caitlin and my friend, Chris; and to the team who help make my professional goals come true – Ann, Sue, Shelley and Chris.

Shine Always, Sue Suchocki – Your Emotionologist™

FOREWORD

In this modern age, children and teens deal with significantly different issues to their ancestors. Yet some issues are the same. Finding where they fit within society can cause children to become anxious and stressed. Children become teens, and their friends become more important than their parents. Relationships are formed, and ways of dealing with conflict are established. Sometimes friendships are tested, and arguments, teasing and bullying occur.

What used to stay in the schoolyard though has changed with the use of technology and instant accessibility; children and teens are no longer able to go home and have a reprieve from peer issues. Technology has meant that not only are arguments filmed and shared online worldwide, but bullying has also extended into the online space. The reputation of a child, teen or adult is ruined with a click of a button and the consequences have led to depression, and for some, to suicide.

The reality is that more than one out of every five students report being bullied. An analysis of 80 studies of both bullying others and being bullied (12-18-year-olds) reported 35% is typical bullying but that 15% occurs online (cyberbullying). Of those bullied online, 90% of teens have also been bullied offline.

Adults are not immune either. Workplace bullying statistics are typically reported around 40% for working adults. Nearly a quarter of high school teachers in New South Wales public schools (Australia) say they have been bullied, primarily by managers or other teachers, in the past year and more than 40% say they have witnessed bullying in that period. This type of bullying is a serious problem.

For a child growing up today, there may literally be no place to escape. Well-meaning teachers and parents often suggest their child and teens should 'build a bridge' or just learn to 'get over it' when they are faced with emotions they cannot process; family members or staff are told that they need to stand up for themselves or become more resilient, but often the question is HOW?

For some time, there has been a need for stress management techniques to be taught in school settings to prepare children with strategies such as meditation and mindfulness being introduced worldwide. The results are promising: students report higher well-being, better social skills and greater academic skills. This development has been encouraging, but there is very little research on why meditation doesn't work in the same way for everyone. It may actually amplify emotional problems that are lying hidden under the surface, and not all people may benefit.

Emotional Freedom Techniques is a new wave of therapeutic approach emerging, which is physically-based with a sound body of evidence and the ability to resolve underlying emotional issues or anxieties. Emotional Freedom Techniques (EFT) is commonly called 'Tapping' because it describes the process itself. Acupressure points on the face and upper body are stimulated in EFT by tapping on them with two or more fingers. This technique may look a little strange, and indeed it has disrupted the therapy space, but the clinical trials are worth reviewing.

In 'The Emotions Behind Bullying Behaviour: Your simple guide to Emotional Freedom Techniques–Tapping!' Sue Suchocki offers a way for our children and teens to process and address the emotions that arise out of situations with bullying. Not only does this book provide a self-applied strategy anyone of any age can use, there is even a chapter on the effects of bullying within the family unit and how to apply EFT to workplace bullying. Bullying extends into many areas of life and adults are not exempt!

Bullying is a complex issue and may need a multi-dimensional approach. This book offers an evidence-based way of managing the distress that arises from bullying at a self-applied level. It is designed for children, teens and adults to use at any time.

With roots in Eastern philosophies, particularly acupuncture, our understanding of how Tapping works has been rapidly progressing. While initial explanations focused on the body's "meridian" or energy system, tapping research now has over a decade of clinical trials which show the tapping technique has profound effects on the nervous system, the production of stress hormones (particularly cortisol), DNA regulation, and brain activation.

A decade-long research program at Harvard Medical School (Boston, USA) examined what happened in the body when various acupuncture points were stimulated and found that certain points on the face and upper body almost instantly decrease the activation of the stress response in the brain (the amygdala). The capacity to rapidly reduce the stress response is a cornerstone in the speed and effectiveness of tapping.

Randomised controlled trials have demonstrated that tapping effectively treats phobias and some anxiety disorders in one session. Several studies show a substantial reduction in Post-Traumatic Stress Disorder / trauma symptoms and often an absence of diagnosis after just 6 hours or sessions of tapping.

Significant decreases in the stress hormone cortisol and normalisation of the EEG frequencies associated with stress also occur after 1 hour and stay changed over time.

Many long-term studies are showing that the changes from tapping last over time. The brain has a unique way to update old learnings, and people who use Tapping may not take their old emotional reactions into the future.

So ultimately, we have this stress management tool – a way of calming the body and brain. Emotional Freedom Techniques may then allow for clearer thoughts and better decision making. Tapping can be used to change distressing or negative feelings, self-limiting thoughts, or behaviours, as well as to instil more positive emotional states, beliefs, or goals. Children and teens who use this technique have reported increased self-esteem, improved self-regulation and reduced difficulties.

Sue has done a superb job in this book of outlining how Tapping can be used for a range of emotions and behaviours related to bullying. Children, teens, teachers and parents will all benefit from reading this. To know you have a way of instantly calming yourself in a moment of distress or heightened emotion is truly freeing, but to know that a child or youth can do the same is even more empowering.

Can you imagine a future where everyone can process their negative emotions as they arise, and students and classrooms regularly use Tapping for stress reduction? This outcome is no longer a distant dream as many classrooms and teachers worldwide have trained in using this technique and indeed use it daily, with many using the technique at home.

A zero-tolerance policy towards bullying, harassment, or abuse of any kind is one thing, but having a proven stress management tool you can use to cope with the effects if it does happen is essential.

Stay open as you read.

Dr Peta Stapleton
Clinical | Health Psychologist | Academic

Author of The Science Behind Tapping: A Proven Stress Management Technique for the Mind and Body

CONTENTS

WHAT IS BULLYING BEHAVIOUR?

"Sticks and stones will break my bones, but names will never hurt me". *The Christian Recorder, 1862.*

Do you know this saying well? Did you say it as a form of defence or was it recited to you by a parent, family member or teacher? Were you just told to "suck it up", "don't let it worry you", "big boys/girls don't cry"? Were you advised to "turn the other cheek" or "stand up for yourself and fight back"?

Today, we know unwanted, repetitive actions and words as bullying, and whether the form is physical, emotional or social, bullying does hurt.

The clinical term to describe a person who uses bullying behaviour is the PERPETRATOR. The clinical term to describe a person who is being bullied is known as the TARGET. You may be more familiar with the words BULLYING or BULLYING BEHAVIOUR, and BULLIED or BEING BULLIED.

It doesn't matter if it is a person who is being bullied by a classmate or friend; a partner, parent or other family members; or an employee who is being bullied by a manager, supervisor or colleague – there are many people impacted by bullying behaviour.

You have a right to feel safe and be treated fairly and respectfully. Bullying is a serious problem with serious mental, physical and social impacts.

THE EMOTIONS BEHIND BULLYING BEHAVIOUR

Let's have a look at the number of personal, social and workplace relationships that are affected by bullying:

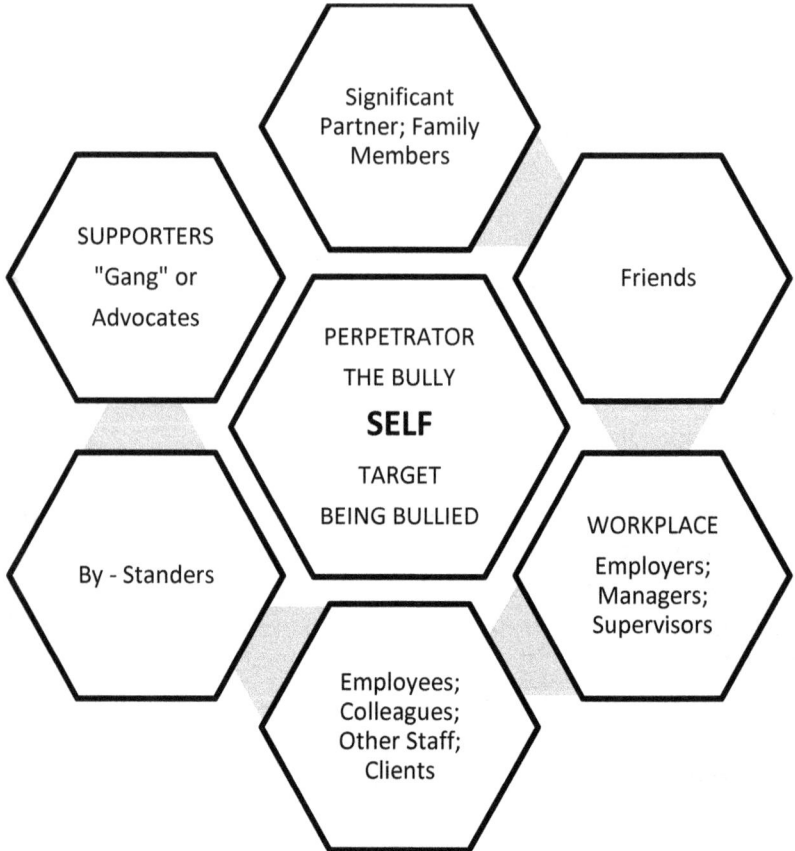

Significant Partner; Family Members

SUPPORTERS "Gang" or Advocates

Friends

PERPETRATOR
THE BULLY

SELF

TARGET
BEING BULLIED

By - Standers

WORKPLACE
Employers;
Managers;
Supervisors

Employees;
Colleagues;
Other Staff;
Clients

PERPETRATOR – The person who carries out harmful acts.
TARGET – The person who is being harmed by those acts.

THE EMOTIONS BEHIND BULLYING BEHAVIOUR

When you see this star ⭐ in this book, it will indicate to you that there is an activity for you to complete.

Think of a time when you felt bullied, or you perhaps thought that you had bullied another person.

⭐ Using your name, their name and the names of those around you who were affected, complete the following chart.

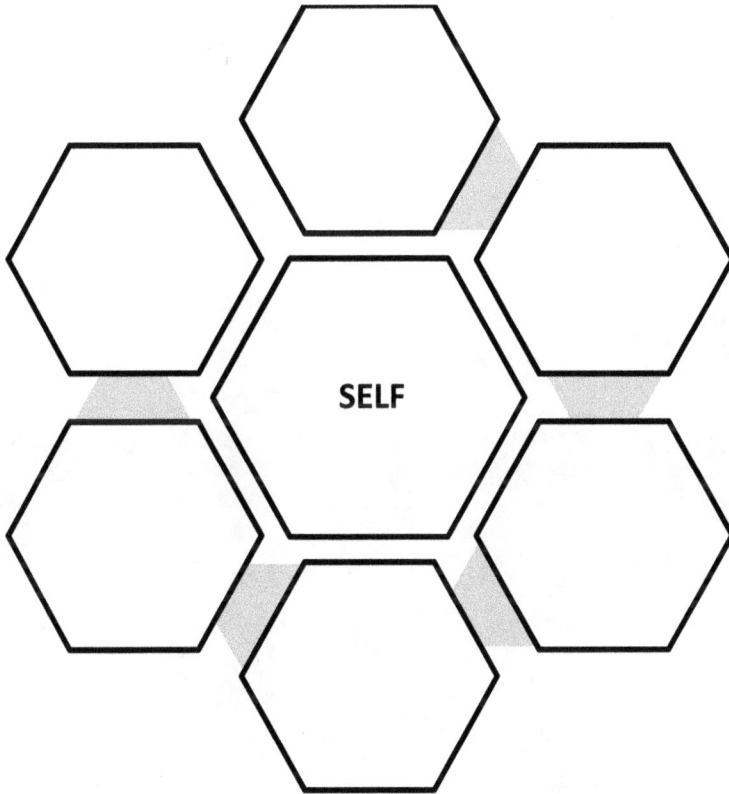

So, the question is, who is hurting?

SECTION 1
THE FACTS BEHIND BULLYING

Although there is no world-wide agreed definition of bullying, there are several defined meanings including the following from Collins Dictionary:

Noun – BULLY
1. A bully is someone who often hurts or frightens other people.

Verb - BULLYING
2. The repeated use of threats or violence in an attempt to harm or intimidate others.

If you look at these definitions, it is clear to see that bullies don't target a person who they perceive as confident. It is not that the target is a weak person, but there is a vulnerability that the bully seeks out and infiltrates. This vulnerability gives the bully some form of power which is used to intimidate or harm another person.

Intelligence gives a person the ability to acquire and apply knowledge and skills. It is the capacity to use brainpower – the power of reasoning, judgement, understanding and perception.

**A perpetrator uses power as a weapon,
creating an imbalance to overpower their target.
From this point on, the terms used in this book will be
BULLY, BULLYING BEHAVIOUR, BULLIED or BEING BULLIED.**

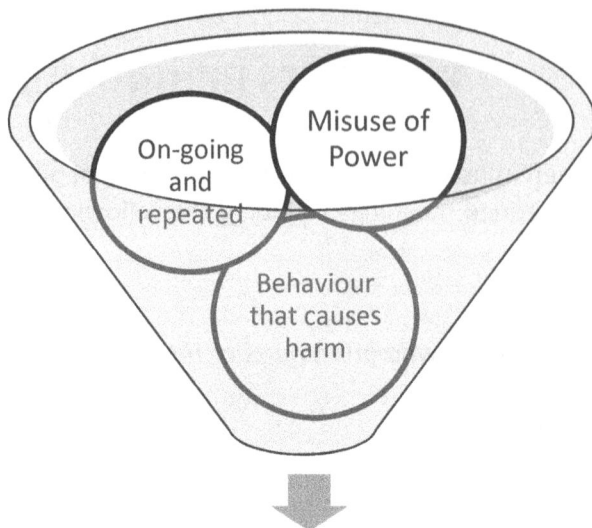

BULLYING BEHAVIOUR

The bully may have some alleged reason to dislike the person, is threatened by the person or feels envious of the person. Perhaps the bully is irritated by another person's beliefs, lifestyle, looks or personality and lashes out in a bullying manner.

The perceived bully might be experiencing pressure or is being bullied from an outside source, so they collect information of value through observation or surveillance that they can use against another person.

The bully may be using their perceived power as a form of defence from their hurts, fears or insecurities. They are using an external control to lessen their anxieties and inner turmoil, pushing away any relationship that makes them feel less in control or inferior.

THE EMOTIONS BEHIND BULLYING BEHAVIOUR

The person being bullied may feel powerless. To counteract this, they may use their EMOTIONAL INTELLIGENCE to become aware of controlling their own EMOTIONS behind the bullying. They can achieve this by handling their thoughts and feelings behind the bullying with the use of EMOTIONAL FREEDOM TECHNIQUES – Tapping! Letting go of their own emotional charges behind being bullied gives the problem or behaviour back to the bully. Stand back and take a look at what the person is getting out of this behaviour of over-powering others.

★ To understand BULLYING BEHAVIOUR, let's take a look at the following questions and ask yourself:

- Is the person so self-absorbed that they don't know that the behaviour they are displaying is bullying?
- Is the person being pressured or bullied by someone who is their superior?
- Is the person so insecure they need to be seen as important or feel accepted by the "gang" that are behind them?
- Has the person been shamed by someone causing them to become isolated, avoid meaningful relationships, self-harm or in the case of a bully, humiliate others by attacking them emotionally, physically or socially protecting themselves?

Bullies may use cowardly behaviours to cause chaos.

They cause chaos within their lives and the lives of others by hiding behind their intimidating behaviour and putting others down to justify their hurt.

It is difficult to feel sympathy for a bully, after all, they are the person hurting others. If you look at the EMOTIONS that are behind the actions of a bully, you can use COGNITIVE EMPATHY by taking a different perspective to bullying. Understanding emotions behind bullying is the first step to "TAPPING OUT NEGATIVITY and TAPPING INTO YOUR HAPPINESS".

BULLYING BEHAVIOUR COVERS FOUR CATEGORIES:
1 – Verbal or Emotional Bullying: This includes localised teasing, name-calling, inappropriate or threatening comments or rumours about a person's lifestyle, looks, personality, disability, gender, sexual preference, race or religion.

2 – Social Bullying: Is interpersonal and happens when someone is trying to hurt another's reputation deliberately. Social bullying includes the spreading of rumours, repeatedly ostracising or turning others against a person or threatens to harm a person or their family.

3 – Physical Bullying: This includes punching, hitting, pushing, spitting, stealing possessions and sexual assault.

4 – Cyberbullying: Cyberbullies use social media to target their victims. Rumours, insults, threats and "dares" can quickly spread through social media. Once on social media, it is difficult to take back or remove comments written.

Oyuys. 2011. *What Is Bullying (And What Isn't Bullying)?*. Accessed February 2019 at www.compassionit.com/2016/02/11/what-is-bullying-and-what-isnt-bullying

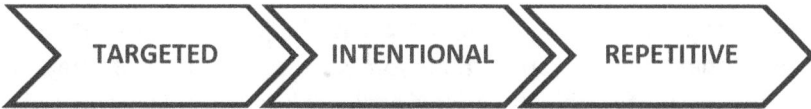

TARGETED ⟫ INTENTIONAL ⟫ REPETITIVE

BULLYING IS NOT:
1 – Excluding someone: It is not considered bullying if a person excludes someone now and then or doesn't invite someone to a particular event. However, repeated and deliberate exclusion within a group setting may be bullying.

2 – Disliking someone: A person may verbally or non-verbally communicate their dislike of another person. This must not include the starting of rumours or verbal abuse of the person.

3 – Accidental physical harm: Unintentionally bumping into another person.

4 – Being "bossy": Constructive criticism delivered respectfully about a person's work, standard or performance review is not considered bullying.

5 – Making a joke with someone (occasionally): While this is not great behaviour, it is not considered bullying unless there are repeated instances.

6 – Arguments: An argument about a subject is not bullying if it is not derogatory of the person or their beliefs.
Ronit. n.d. *What is NOT bullying?*. Accessed February 2019 at www.ronitbaras.com/emotional-intelligence/personal-development/what-is-not-bullying/

Sometimes you may categorise certain behaviours as bullying when they are not deliberate or repetitive. Conflict is not always bullying if it is handled with fairness.

The occasional teasing, being the brunt of a joke or being made to feel embarrassed by something someone did or said can make a person uncomfortable or sad but again, this is not bullying.

Sarcasm is another form of teasing that is often missed by some people who can't understand the intonation, pitch or stressing of words, which turns a simple statement into a sarcastic comment. The words "Oh, thanks" in a normal voice is a compliment, while the words "Ohh, thaanks" said more slowly or through the nose while you are contorting your face would be thought to be meant as being sarcastic. ★ Go on, try it!

Sarcasm is also tricky to pick up in a text or on social media as you are not able to hear the intention behind the wording, so what might seem funny to one person, hurts another person.

In the first instance, letting the person know that you are not comfortable with what they just did or that it is not OK to talk to you in that way is generally all that is needed to stop generalised teasing.

An individual's perception makes the definition of bullying a difficult line to put in the sand. It is actions that are intentional, repetitive and hurtful that can cause a person to become sad, angry, withdrawn or depressed.

When it comes to coping with being bullied, the word "RESILIENCE" is very often used. Resilience is the capacity to recover quickly from difficulties or having a toughness. While being resilient is an important characteristic to get a person through life's difficulties, it is not enough to expect a person who is being bullied to "toughen up" to this bullying behaviour.

THE EMOTIONS BEHIND BULLYING BEHAVIOUR

In saying this, some areas of resilience training are essential to support the person being bullied. Examples might include:

- Building a support network;
- Learning skills to make your situation better;
- Keeping a positive outlook on your strengths;
- Recognising your good qualities or what you like to do;
- Keeping your reactions to a situation in perspective.

★ Name 5 people who make up a part of your support network.

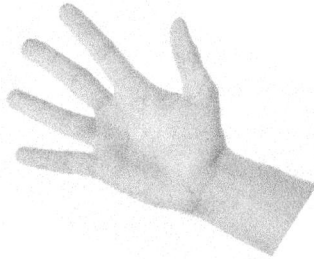

The EMOTIONAL FREEDOM TECHNIQUES – Tapping! shared with you in the following sections is an easy to learn self-help technique to safely manage your negative emotions behind the bullying behaviour or being bullied.

SECTION 2
TAPPING INTO YOUR HAPPINESS

Bullying behaviour or being bullied may affect how you feel about yourself.

Let's have a look at your "smart"! Are you good with words, numbers, drawing, sports or dance? Do you have a good ear for music, exceptional people skills or a love of nature?

LET'S TAKE A "SELFIE" ABOUT HOW SMART YOU ARE:

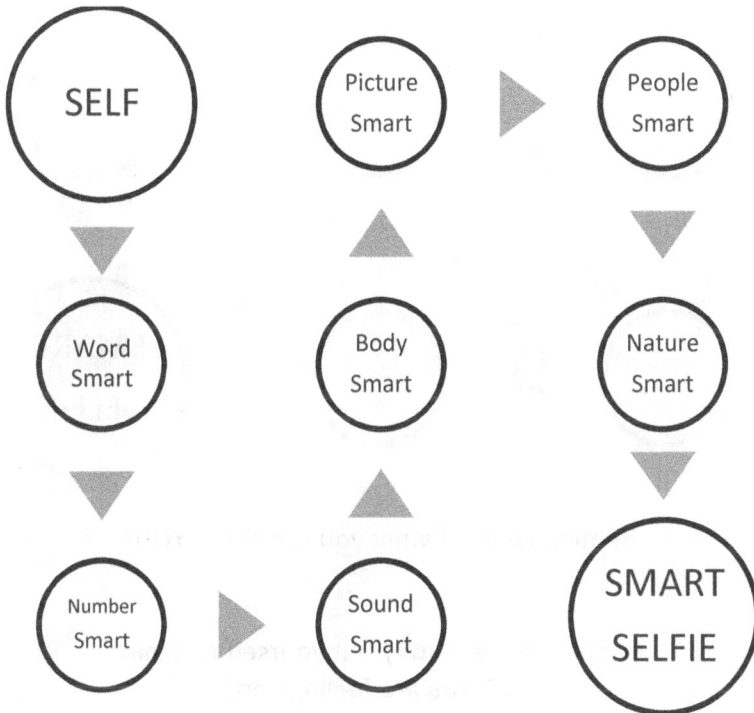

SELF

Picture Smart → People Smart

Word Smart

Body Smart

Nature Smart

Number Smart → Sound Smart

SMART SELFIE

You don't need to be "perfect" or good at everything; you just need to be "enough".

★ Pick out your strengths and write down what you like most about your abilities in each area.

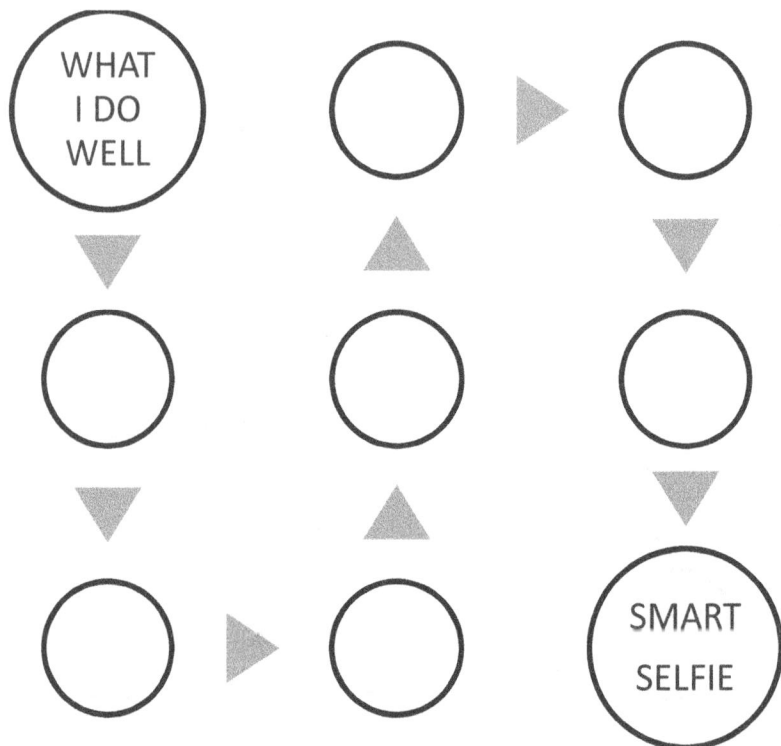

WHAT
I DO
WELL

SMART

SELFIE

Remind yourself what you like about YOU!

**It's hard to feel bad about yourself or others
when you are feeling good!**

★ SECTION 3
THE THEORY BEHIND TAPPING

In this section you will discover that EMOTIONAL FREEDOM TECHNIQUES-Tapping! is a way of identifying NEGATIVE EMOTIONS behind the issue and dealing with those EMOTIONS for one last time.

EFT-Tapping! is detecting and facing fears in a safe way, whether they be a lack of control or self-worth, stress, anxiety, shame, guilt, envy, phobias, abuse, pressure from an outside source or other physical or emotional events throughout your life. Dr Peta Stapleton, PhD., Researcher of Evidence Based EFT, has identified the following three clinical theories used in Emotional Freedom Techniques:

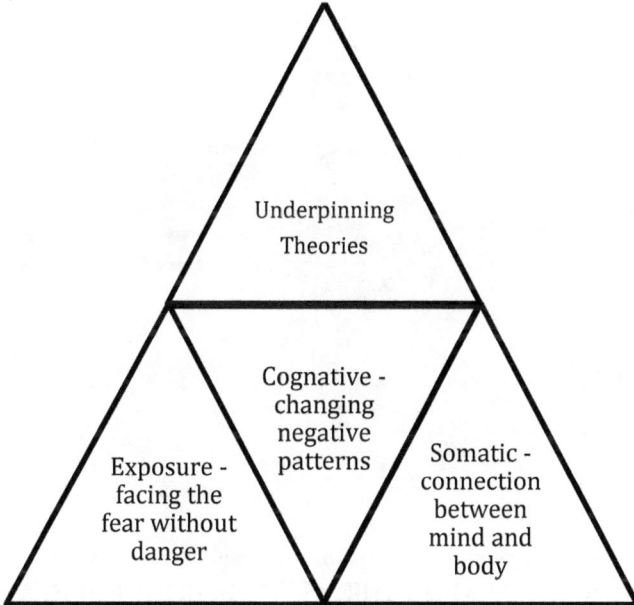

As part of the EFT-Tapping! process, you will INVESTIGATE your PROBLEM or ISSUE and identify key words which are used in the TAPPING process. These words may challenge your negative thought patterns or limiting beliefs and change the effects on the limbic system in your brain which controls your EMOTIONS, behaviour and motivation.

The TAPPING technique is done by using your fingertips to perform a SEQUENCE of gentle TAPPING on the SIDE OF HAND, followed by TAPPING a ROUND on the face and upper body. This process will be explained in the following sections.

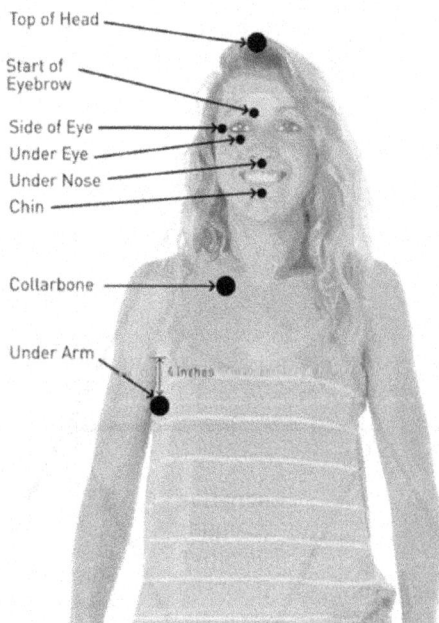

Top of Head
Start of Eyebrow
Side of Eye
Under Eye
Under Nose
Chin
Collarbone
Under Arm
4 inches

EFT images printed with permission from Dr Peta Stapleton
"WHAT YOUR MIND THINKS, YOUR BODY FOLLOWS."

THE EMOTIONS BEHIND BULLYING BEHAVIOUR

★ Imagine you are holding a lemon. Imagine holding it in your hand, turning it around, looking at it and smelling it.

Now, imagine cutting the lemon open, squeezing it so that the juice is starting to drip out. Lick the lemon, bite off a piece and hold it in your mouth.

What reaction are you displaying in your mouth right at this moment?

Do you feel that your saliva has built up? Yes! Your brain is telling you that you need saliva for your teeth to chew food and to help with digestion. Just thinking about eating a lemon started this process.

Your mind works in the same way when it comes to your EMOTIONS. Just like the reaction to the imaginary lemon, your brain can't distinguish between real or imagined threats. Instinctively, your mind automatically sets off your SYMPATHETIC NERVOUS SYSTEM, activating rapid emotional, psychological, and physical changes to your body.

Following your natural survival instincts was helpful when chased by a bear or fighting for your survival, but in today's world, these responses are set off by non-life-threatening triggers, causing you to respond to life's stresses in 4 ways:

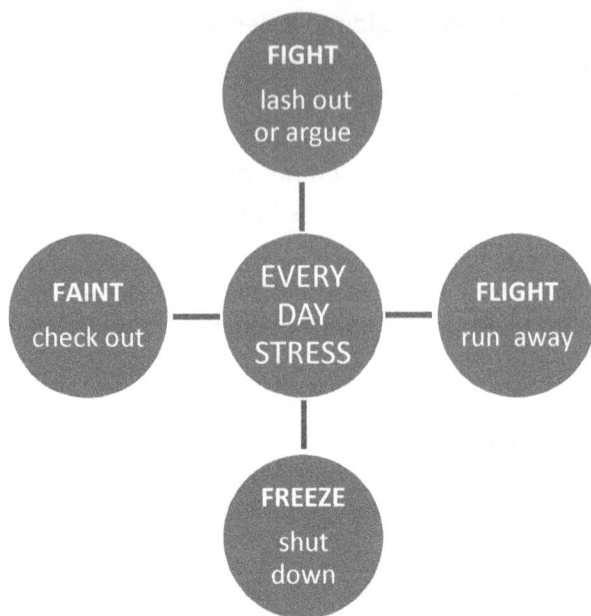

THE BEGINNINGS OF EMOTIONAL FREEDOM TECHNIQUES:

Dr Roger Callahan, PhD., clinical psychologist and founder of Thought Field Therapy, first used the idea of tapping on points on the body while working with a client named Mary, who was suffering from a phobia of water. Her symptoms consisted of headaches and nightmares related to her phobia. She had tried several treatments over the years, but there didn't seem to be any improvement.

Dr Callahan wasn't having much luck with Mary's phobia either. Mary was also complaining of feeling sick in the stomach.

At this time, Dr Callahan had been studying the body's ENERGY SYSTEM and "TAPPED" with his fingertips on Mary's face on an ACUPRESSURE POINT under her eye that he knew was related to stomach issues.

Mary began to feel less sick in the stomach, with an added benefit: Mary announced that her phobia was gone, and she ran to the swimming pool in Dr Callahan's garden and started to throw water on her face! During a follow-up session, Mary stated that she no longer had headaches or nightmares about water.

Dr Callahan continued to fine-tune the TAPPING POINTS, finding the technique worked on many other physical and emotional ISSUES.

Gary Craig, an engineer who trained at Stanford, studied the technique developed by Dr Callahan and over the years has further refined the points that we use today in Emotional Freedom Techniques.

These Emotional Freedom Techniques make up what is now known as the "DISCOVERY STATEMENT".

The statement isn't saying that past events cause your EMOTIONS, but that your thoughts behind these events are sending out an electrical charge, creating the NEGATIVE EMOTIONS.
Gary C.; Tina C. 1995. *What is EFT?*. Accessed February 2019 at
https://www.emofree.com/eft-tutorial/tapping-basics/what-is-eft.html

**"THE CAUSE OF ALL NEGATIVE EMOTIONS IS
A DISRUPTION IN THE BODY'S ENERGY SYSTEM."**

EFT-Tapping! uses a gentle technique to quickly relieve both PHYSICAL ASPECTS and EMOTIONAL ISSUES including anxiety, grief, fear, unhealthy desires and self-worth and associated ISSUES, and phobias behind these PROBLEMS. EFT-Tapping! doesn't take away natural emotions, make you forget the issue, or lessen the severity of the event. It stops the EMOTIONAL RESPONSES that cause NEGATIVE REACTIONS or EMOTIONS.

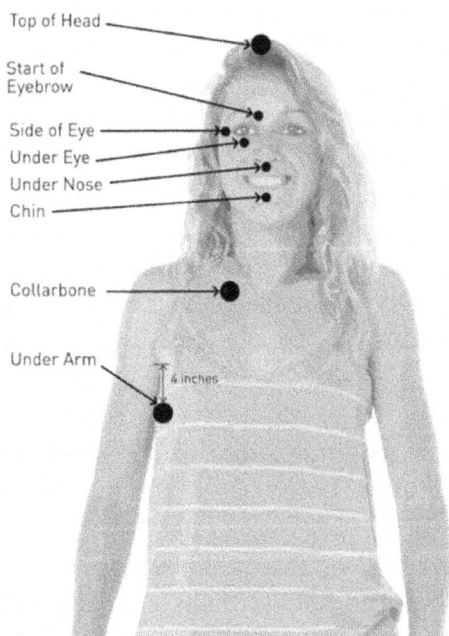

Top of Head
Start of Eyebrow
Side of Eye
Under Eye
Under Nose
Chin
Collarbone
Under Arm
4 inches

EFT images printed with permission from Dr Peta Stapleton

EFT-Tapping! allows you to acknowledge your negative emotions by tapping on points on your hand, face and upper body and let go of these emotions once and for all, rather than sweeping your emotions under the carpet.

★ SECTION 4
YOUR RECIPE FOR TAPPING

In this section you will become familiar with the TAPPING POINTS on your hand, face and upper body.

EMOTIONAL FREEDOM TECHNIQUES-Tapping! can be used on all emotional problems including the fear, anger, grief and guilt brought on by social, emotional, physical or performance bullying.

EFT-Tapping! is a simple to use self-care technique to keep in your emotional toolbox. You can use EFT-Tapping! anywhere and apply it to any ISSUE.

In the following sections, you will be shown an EFT-Tapping! BASIC RECIPE or method, and learn how to find the words you will say while TAPPING on POINTS to release your NEGATIVE EMOTIONS.

EFT-Tapping! begins with a SET-UP STATEMENT SEQUENCE which uses the soft fleshy part at the SIDE OF HAND known as your KARATE CHOP point; or FRIENDLY SPOT for EFT-Tapping! with kids.

This SET-UP STATEMENT SEQUENCE is followed by an EFT-Tapping! ROUND which uses 8 of the 12 meridians and 2 governing vessels from Eastern teachings. As the points are interconnected, they send balancing energy down one pathway, influencing other pathways within the body.

The illustrations below, together with the written explanations of each point, will help you to find each of the TAPPING POINTS on your face and upper body.

★ For now, locate each of these TAPPING POINTS on your body and touch each of them using the tips of your pointer and middle fingers.

HOW TO FIND YOUR SIDE OF HAND or KARATE CHOP POINT.

KC: The **KARATE CHOP** point or **SIDE OF HAND** point – is located at the centre of the fleshy part of the outside of either of your hands, between the top of the wrist and the base of the little finger or, stated differently, the part of your hand you would use to deliver a karate chop.

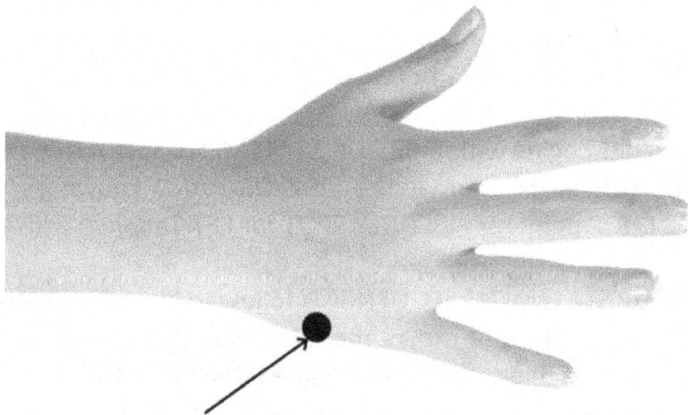

Side of the Hand

EFT images printed with permission from Dr Peta Stapleton

The Side of Hand or Karate Chop point is used as part of the set-up statement sequence by tapping on it continuously.

HOW TO FIND YOUR TAPPING POINTS.

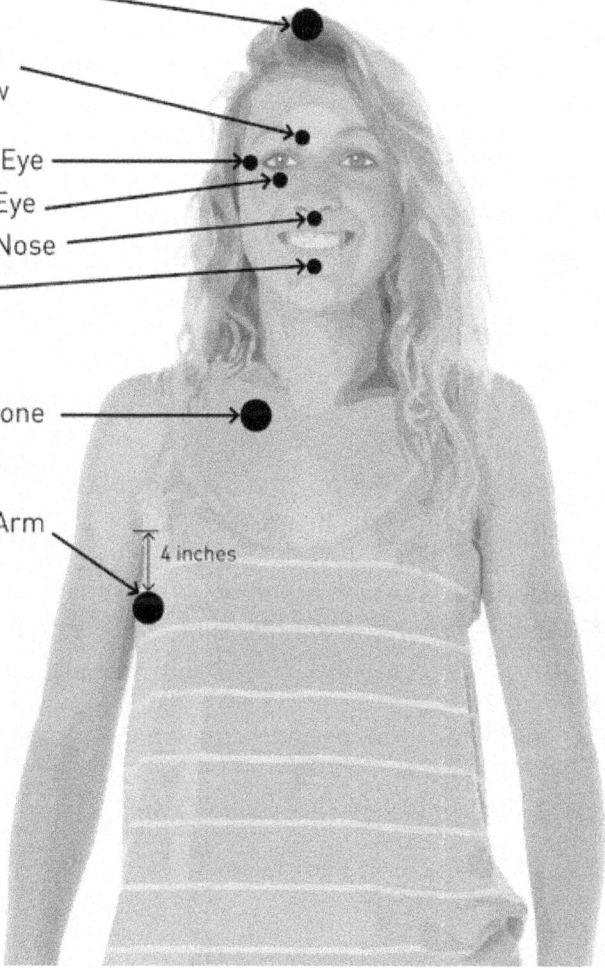

Top of Head

Start of
Eyebrow

Side of Eye

Under Eye

Under Nose

Chin

Collarbone

Under Arm

4 inches

EFT images printed with permission from Dr Peta Stapleton

EB: EYEBROW - the beginning of the eyebrow, where it meets the nose.

SE: SIDE OF EYE - the bone bordering the outside corner of the eye.

UE: UNDER EYE - the bone under an eye below and in line with your pupil.

UN: UNDER NOSE - the small area between the bottom of your nose and the top of your upper lip.

CH: CHIN - midway between the point of your chin and the bottom of your lower lip.

CB: COLLARBONE - first place your pointer finger on the U-shaped notch at the top of the breastbone, about where a man would knot his tie. From the bottom of the U, move your pointer finger down 2.5 cm and then go to the left (or right) 2.5 cm. Note: This point is below the collarbone, not on or above the collarbone. It is *not* the point that is also known as the "SORE SPOT".

UA: UNDER ARM - the side of the body, at a point in line with the nipple (for men) or on the top of the bra strap on the side of your body (for women). It is about 10 cm below the armpit.

ToH: TOP of HEAD - draw a line from one ear, over the head, to the other ear, and another line from your nose to the back of your neck, the ToH point is where those two lines would intersect.

For simplicity all tapping points use abbreviations.
EB; SE; UE; UN; CH; CB; UA; ToH.

★ SECTION 5
YOUR BASIC RECIPE – UTENSILS

In this section you will find that the SIDE OF HAND or KARATE CHOP point is generally only used as part of the SET-UP STATEMENT SEQUENCE that you will learn later. This TAPPING POINT helps your brain acknowledge that even though you have this PROBLEM, you are willing to, or are choosing to try to accept yourself just the way you are as a person.

★ Using all your fingers on one hand, continuously TAP the SIDE OF HAND or KARATE CHOP point on your other hand. No, it doesn't matter which side you use! Oh, that tingles!

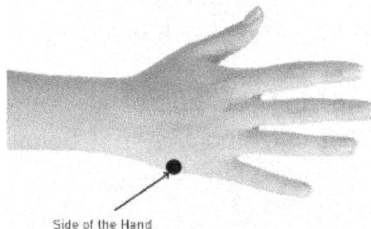

Side of the Hand

For each TAPPING POINT during a ROUND you can use two or more fingers. Some TAPPING POINTS you will find that you use all your fingers and thumb to ensure that you are getting the correct spot. The recommended fingers to use are explained below.

It doesn't matter which hand you use, which side of your face or body you TAP on, or if you use one or two hands or swap hands. If you miss a TAPPING POINT during a ROUND, you can catch it up on the next ROUND. The pressure of the TAPPING is firm enough to feel but soft enough not to hurt. You can't do anything wrong, just keep TAPPING!

HOW TO TAP.

⭐ **EYEBROW** - Using two fingers, pointer and middle fingers, find the point at the inside point of your eyebrow where it touches your nose, TAP 5 to 8 times.

⭐ **SIDE OF EYE** - Using pointer and middle fingers, find the point on the bone at the side of your eye, TAP 5 to 8 times.

⭐ **UNDER EYE** - Following the bone around to under the pupil, using pointer and middle fingers, TAP 5 to 8 times.

⭐ **UNDER NOSE** - Using pointer and middle fingers, TAP 5 to 8 times on the "divot" between your nose and your top lip.

⭐ **CHIN** - Using pointer and middle fingers, TAP 5 to 8 times on the crease of your chin below your bottom lip.

⭐ **COLLARBONE** - Using the tips of all your fingers and your thumb OR make a fist and find the spot below your collarbone, TAPPING or gentle thumping 5 to 8 times.

⭐ **UNDER ARM** - Using 4 fingers or a "flat" hand and lifting one arm up, take the other arm across your body in line with your nipple, TAP 5 to 8 times. Alternatively, you can raise each elbow and TAP on the same side of your body with that hand - like a monkey scratching!

⭐ **TOP of HEAD** - Using the tips of your fingers and your thumb TAP on the top of your head 5 to 8 times.

A relaxing way to finish the round is to take a nice deep breath in and let it out while gently clasping either wrist.

Top of Head

Start of
Eyebrow

Side of Eye

Under Eye

Under Nose

Chin

Collarbone

Under Arm

4 inches

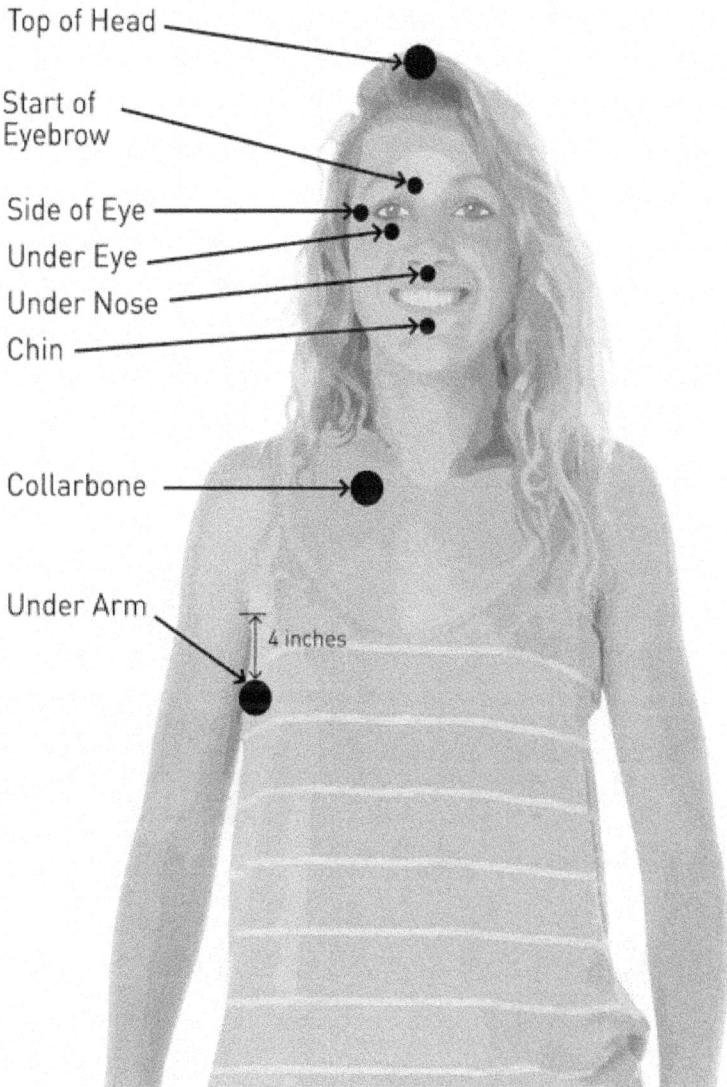

EFT images printed with permission from Dr Peta Stapleton.

SECTION 6
YOUR BASIC RECIPE – INGREDIENTS

In this section you will uncover what makes up the EFT-Tapping! BASIC RECIPE – the method you will use! Like many good recipes, it is essential to follow the BASIC RECIPE in the order written.

Water is a conductor of energy, so while you are practising EFT– Tapping! make sure to drink plenty of water. You will find by using the right method, ingredients and measurements, you can create a BASIC RECIPE that you can follow. More details on how to use the method is explained in the next section.

THE FIVE BASIC INGREDIENTS:

1. Investigate your **PROBLEM**.
2. Guess your **SUBJECTIVE UNIT OF DISTRESS – SUD's** score.
3. Create a **SET-UP STATEMENT** by **TAPPING** the **SIDE OF HAND** while **REPEATING THE STATEMENT** aloud x **3**.
4. **TAP** on each of the 8 individual **TAPPING POINTS** while saying your **REMINDER PHRASE** to complete a **ROUND**.
5. Take a BREATH IN and OUT. Re-rate your SUD's score.

Repeat STEPS 4 & 5 and watch your problem lessen until your SUD's score is neutral or "0", or the problem just doesn't seem to worry you as much anymore.

SECTION 7
YOUR BASIC RECIPE – METHOD

1. Identify what your PROBLEM is and what EMOTIONS are behind your current feelings about this PROBLEM:
   My Problem: (Hurt by my sister in front of my friend)
   My Emotions: (Hurt, Embarrassed, Stupid, Worthless)

2. Guess the RATE of your SUBJECTIVE UNIT OF DISTRESS:
   Your SUD's score is how strongly you feel the EMOTION.
   10 - really intense
   8 - intense
   6 - annoying
   4 - slightly annoying
   2 - irritating
   0 - neutral
   My SUD's score: "7"

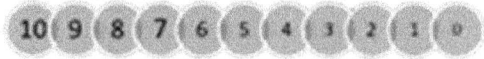

3. Create a SET-UP STATEMENT SEQUENCE by asking yourself:
   What is the strongest emotion I am feeling?
   Who is the person, or self, associated with this feeling?
   What happened to me to feel this way?

   My SET-UP STATEMENT SEQUENCE.
   TAP SIDE OF HAND while saying the following three times:
   Even though I feel (hurt)
   By (my sister)
   For (putting me down in front of my friend)

   I deeply and completely accept myself; or
   I'm OK as a person; or I choose to let this (hurt) go.

4. Your REMINDER PHRASE is a short phrase which is said aloud while you are TAPPING, 5 to 8 times on each TAPPING POINT to complete a ROUND. Your REMINDER PHRASE helps you to stay focused on your EMOTIONAL trigger.

My REMINDER PHRASES:
> *(This hurt)*
> *(Sooo hurt)*
> *(I felt so hurt)*
> *(Hurt by my sister)*
> *(My sister hurt me)*
> *(Embarrassed by my sister)*
> *(I was sooo embarrassed)*
> *(Embarrassed in front of my friends)*

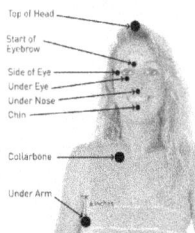

5. After completing one or more TAPPING ROUNDS, *take a BREATH IN and OUT,* guess a number to *RE-RATE your SUD's* score to test if you still feel as strongly about the EMOTION.
> *My SUD's score: "4"*

REPEAT STEPS 4 & 5 of the BASIC RECIPE, **BREATH IN and OUT** until your SUBJECTIVE LEVEL DISTRESS (SUD's) is NEUTRAL, "0", or you feel OK and the problem is no longer worrying you.
> *My SUD's score: "0"*

10 9 8 7 6 5 4 3 2 1 0

SIMPLE ISN'T IT! Like all good bakers, it will take some practise to get the right consistency and to do it without having to look at the basic recipe.

SECTION 8
INVESTIGATING YOUR PROBLEM

In this section you will be INVESTIGATING your PROBLEM to help you to identify the important ISSUE and EMOTIONS behind this problem. By answering the following questions with one or two of your strongest memories, feelings or sensations, you will get to the CORE ISSUE of your PROBLEM.

THE TIME WHEN:
   (At 15, sister made fun of me in front of my friend)

➢ **WHO –**   Was involved: *(me, sister, friend)*

➢ **SEE –**   Places/Room: *(at the mall)*

➢ **WHAT –** Expressions did you notice: *(gloating)*

➢ **HEAR –** Sounds/Words: *(you're not as pretty as me; no-one will ever go out with you; you're so ugly; bitch)*

➢ **WHAT –** Tone of voice was used: *(snickering, snarling)*

➢ **SMELLS–** Distinct odours if any: *(cheap body spray)*

➢ **TASTES –**Actual or perceived if any: *(bad taste)*

➢ **FEEL –**   Emotions experienced: *(hurt, sadness, stupidity, worthlessness, embarrassed)*

➢ **THINK –** To self: *(That's not very kind; I'm heartbroken; Why is she trying to hurt me? Maybe she's right)*

➢ **WHERE –**Did you feel the emotions physically: *(tummy, chest)*

33

THE EMOTIONS BEHIND BULLYING BEHAVIOUR

➢ **HOW** – Are you carrying these emotions:

    Physically in your body – *(sick feeling in stomach)*

    Emotional well-being – *(withdrawn, not confident)*

➢ **WHY** – Are you holding on to these emotions or what are you getting out of them by holding on to them:

    (self-protection)

The last question in our investigation is interesting and is relevant, especially if there is any form of resistance to EFT-Tapping!

The term used for holding on to these emotions is PSYCHOLOGICAL REVERSAL, which is a subconscious condition of self-sabotage—that is, making choices that bring you misery instead of the well-being and the happiness you say you want.

In the past, this effect has been likened to putting batteries in your torchlight the wrong way. The light won't work because of polar reversal. Basically, you are holding on to your ISSUE or EMOTIONS because you are getting a SECONDARY GAIN from it.

A SECONDARY GAIN may be used because of:

- Protection – it is not safe to let this go;
- Uncertainty or fear - who would I be without this issue;
- Victory - if I let go of this issue, "they" will win;
- Or it may just be a "good STORY" that you gain special attention or notoriety from – might be feeling vulnerable.

THE EMOTIONS BEHIND BULLYING BEHAVIOUR

A SECONDARY GAIN may include:

- Having a sore knee means not having to do exercise;
- Back pain while not working means compo to live on;
- Not losing weight, so you don't attract unwanted romantic attention;
- Not starting a new career path, in case you fail again.

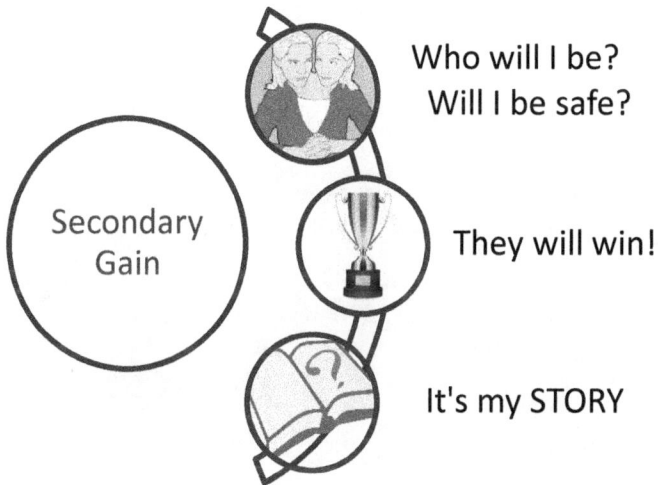

Secondary Gain

Who will I be?
Will I be safe?

They will win!

It's my STORY

**A secondary gain generally gives you a reason or "excuse"
not to try to resolve your problem even when you
are saying that is what you want.**

SECTION 9
THE INTENSITY BEHIND EMOTIONS

In this section you will be shown how to guess your SUBJECTIVE UNIT OF DISTRESS or SUD's score to RATE the INTENSITY or "how bad" your problem is. Your SUD's score uses self-estimation on a scale of "10 to 0" with "10" = INTENSE down to "0" = NEUTRAL of EMOTIONAL INTENSITY.

In EMOTIONAL FREEDOM TECHNIQUES-Tapping!, you RATE each PROBLEM before you do your first SET-UP STATEMENT SEQUENCE which includes TAPPING on your SIDE OF HAND, while saying your STATEMENT aloud 3 times.

You RE-RATE your SUD's score after you complete one or more TAPPING ROUNDS to see how much progress you are making.

For your first SUD's score, you will RATE the amount of discomfort that your PROBLEM or the EMOTION behind your problem is causing you at this moment, whether this is an emotional or physical pain.

10 = INTENSE feelings　　　　　　　　**0 = NEUTRAL feelings**

10 9 8 7 6 5 4 3 2 1 0

**You may find that it takes a few tapping rounds for your SUD's score to drop down, or you may find that they go up!
This is ok. Look at your words to see if they are how you are feeling. If not, change your words and tap another round.**

★ SUBJECTIVE UNIT OF DISTRESS or SUD's score is a subjective measurement that is based on your personal feelings. This exercise will help you to understand scoring your SUD's. Guess the INTENSITY out of 10, with "10" being the worse and "0" being OK for the following events:

Scenario	Rating
You are running late for an important meeting or exam.	
Your friend didn't notice your new hairstyle.	
Your sister laughed at you in front of everyone for getting the answer to a question wrong.	
Your boss humiliated you in front of other staff.	
A family member yelled and swore at you for not doing the washing up "good enough".	

10 9 8 7 6 5 4 3 2 1 0

Remember, EMOTIONAL FREEDOM TECHNIQUES-Tapping! is about YOUR THOUGHTS, EMOTIONS or FEELINGS, so each person may have a different SUD's score to the same event.

In EFT-Tapping!, there are no wrong answers! Not all events need to be a catastrophe or have a high SUD's score to use EFT-Tapping! on them.

It is easy to clear a problem that has a lower intensity, although with EFT-Tapping! by clearing the larger problem, you will find that the smaller problems collapse naturally.

Another way of measuring your INTENSITY level is by using HAND MEASUREMENTS – wide apart for INTENSE feelings / close together for NEUTRAL feelings.

This form of measurement is especially useful for people who can't put a SUBJECTIVE UNIT OF DISTRESS (SUD's) number on their NEGATIVE EMOTIONS or for children to indicate their LEVEL OF DISTRESS or "how big" their PROBLEM or EMOTION behind their problem is.

10 9 8 7 6 5 4 3 2 1 0

Finding your SUD's score will become more natural if you firstly focus on the feeling like anger, sadness, hurt, fear etc. and then ask yourself how much this feeling is bothering you at this time.

SECTION 10
STORY BEHIND YOUR EMOTIONS

In this section you will understand the importance of identifying your PROBLEM or ISSUE and to be as SPECIFIC as you can about how you felt about it for results that are TERRIFIC!

The thought process behind EMOTIONAL FREEDOM TECHNIQUES-Tapping! is perhaps entirely different to your current way of thinking. With EFT-Tapping! you will be doing the opposite of what you may be used to. With EFT-Tapping! you are remembering, acknowledging and accepting the NEGATIVE EMOTIONS behind your story rather than the EVENT. You deal with those NEGATIVE EMOTIONS by TAPPING on acupressure points while accepting yourself as a person and the good within you.

By acknowledging and accepting the NEGATIVE EMOTIONS behind your problem, while using EFT-Tapping! you are giving yourself permission to let go of your PROBLEM once and for all.

If the ISSUE is too deep, the following GENTLE TAPPING method can be used by TAPPING on just the NAME of your STORY which should be general enough only have an intensity of "5" or less until your SUD's level drops to a point where you can TAP without feeling too distressed.

If your story becomes overwhelming and you start to cry, keep tapping without words with your eyes open until you feel calmer and can continue with your story.

THE EMOTIONS BEHIND BULLYING BEHAVIOUR

1. IDENTIFY and NAME YOUR STORY: by putting an ending to these words: *The time when:*

_____

2. RATE SUD's score: if your SUD's is too high, TAP only on the NAME of your STORY until the INTENSITY has decreased and you feel comfortable using words from your investigation.

10 9 8 7 6 5 4 3 2 1 0

My SUD's score: "5"

3. SET-UP STATEMENT SEQUENCE:
Even though I have this story that is too difficult to talk about, I deeply and completely accept myself.
Even though I have this scary story,
I deeply and completely accept myself.
Even though I don't think I can ever tell my story,
I deeply and completely accept myself.

4. TAPPING ROUNDS and REMINDER PHRASES:

EB -	*My story;*
SE -	*This story;*
UE -	*My story;*
UN -	*My scary story;*
CH -	*My story;*
CB -	*This story;*
UA -	*This difficult story;*
ToH -	*I don't think I can tell this story;*

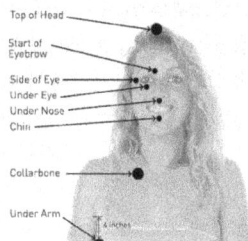

Top of Head
Start of Eyebrow
Side of Eye
Under Eye
Under Nose
Chin
Collarbone
Under Arm

5. Take a BREATH IN and OUT then RE-RATE SUD's score:

10 9 8 7 6 5 4 3 2 1 0

My SUD's score: "*4*"

REPEAT STEPS 4 & 5 of the BASIC RECIPE, take a BREATH IN and OUT, RE-RATE your SUD's until it is 5 or less.

My SUD's score: "*3*"

Now, you can start to bring in the actual words and emotions from your investigations as your REMINDER PHRASES to replace the phrase "this STORY" in your TAPPING ROUND.

REPEAT STEPS 4 & 5 of the BASIC RECIPE, take a BREATH IN and OUT, RE-RATE your SUD's.

My SUD's score: "*4*"

REPEAT STEPS 4 & 5 of the BASIC RECIPE, take a BREATH IN and OUT, RE-RATE your SUD's.

My SUD's score: "*1*"

REPEAT STEPS 4 & 5 of the BASIC RECIPE, take a BREATH IN and OUT, RE-RATE your SUD's until it is NEUTRAL or "0".

**Let go of the hurt and the pain once and for all!
Carrying around this hurt is not doing you any good
emotionally or physically.**

★ SECTION 11
YOUR FINAL PRODUCT

In this section you will learn how EMOTIONAL FREEDOM TECHNIQUES-Tapping! can work for you. Maybe you have doubts that you won't know what to say. Just follow the BASIC RECIPE.

A few doubts, when trying something new, are healthy. Let's look at an example of investigating EFT-Tapping! The PROBLEM is some DOUBT, and you can hear your family saying, "Tapping isn't going to work for you." This example gives you the opportunity to add your own words, feelings and thoughts if you would like to.

- ➤ **WHO –**   Was involved: *Me, Sue the author, partner/family*
- ➤ **SEE –**   Places/Room: *in your bedroom*
- ➤ **WHAT –**   Expressions did you notice: *screwed up nose*
- ➤ **HEAR –**   Sounds/Words: *Why are you even trying this? It won't work for you. It's just the way you are. It's stupid!*
- ➤ **WHAT –**   Tone of voice: *put downs, scepticism*
- ➤ **SMELLS –** Distinct odours if any: *smell of the book pages*
- ➤ **TASTES –** Actual or perceived if any: *bad taste, salty tears*
- ➤ **FEEL –**   Emotions experienced: *sadness, scared, silly, failure*
- ➤ **THINK –**   To self: *Why am I doing this! I don't think it will work. What will my family think if I fail? Can I trust Sue? Nothing works.*
- ➤ **WHERE –** Did you feel the emotions physically: *stomach, eyes*
- ➤ **HOW –**   Are you carrying these emotions:
  Physically in your body – *sinking feeling in tummy, crying*
  Emotional well-being – *giving up, withdrawn*

➢ **WHY –** Are you holding on to these emotions or what are you getting out of them by holding on to them: _an excuse not to try EFT-Tapping! In case it doesn't work, or I fail at it!_

1. IDENTIFY and NAME your STORY:
   The time when: I DOUBTED EFT-Tapping! would work.

Notice what your PROBLEM is and what EMOTIONS are behind this current feeling about this PROBLEM. These are the words you picked out from your investigation:
   My Problem: Doubt EFT-Tapping! will work for me
   My Emotions: Scared, Silly, Failure

2. Guess the RATE of your SUBJECTIVE UNIT OF DISTRESS:
   Your SUD's score for how strongly you feel about the DOUBT.

   10 9 8 7 6 5 4 3 2 1 0

   My SUD's score: _____

3. Create a SET-UP STATEMENT SEQUENCE by asking yourself:
   What is the strongest emotion I am feeling?
   Who is the person, or self, associated with this feeling?
   What happened to me to feel this way?

   My SET-UP STATEMENT SEQUENCE.
   TAP SIDE OF HAND while saying the following three times:
   Even though I feel DOUBTFUL within myself
   That EFT Tapping will work for me,

   I deeply and completely accept myself;
   I will be OK; I am willing to giving it a try.

4. Your REMINDER PHRASE is a very short phrase which is said aloud while you are TAPPING, 5 to 8 times on each of the 8 TAPPING POINTS to complete a ROUND. Your REMINDER PHRASE helps you to stay focused on what triggered your NEGATIVE EMOTIONS.

My REMINDER PHRASES:

EYEBROW -	*I doubt if this EFT will work*
SIDE of EYE -	*I'm scared to use it*
UNDER EYE -	*It won't work for me*
UNDER NOSE -	*What if I can't do it?*
CHIN -	*It all seems a bit silly*
COLLARBONE -	*I won't know what to say/do*
UNDER ARM -	*Nothing ever works for me*
TOP of HEAD -	*I doubt if this tapping will work*

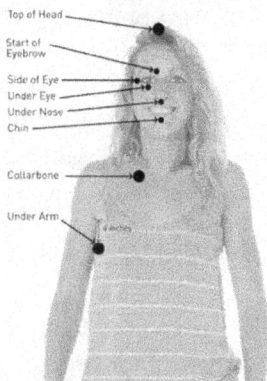

EFT images printed with permission from Dr Peta Stapleton

5. After completing one or more TAPPING ROUNDS saying your REMINDER PHRASES, take a BREATH IN and OUT and then guess a number to RE-RATE your SUD's score to TEST how strongly you still feel about the DOUBT.

My SUD's score: _____

My REMINDER PHRASES:

EB -	*I doubt if this EFT will work*
SE -	*I'm scared to use it*
UE -	*It won't work for me*
UN -	*What if I can't do it?*
CH -	*It all seems a bit silly*
CB -	*I won't know what to say/do*
UA -	*Nothing ever works for me*
ToH -	*I doubt if tapping will work*

REPEAT STEPS 4 & 5 of the BASIC RECIPE, take a BREATH IN and OUT, RE-RATE your SUD's score behind the DOUBT you feel about EFT-Tapping! working for you until it gets below "4".

RE-RATE SUD's score: _____

NEW SET-UP STATEMENT if stuck on low SUD's score:

Even though for whatever reason, I don't want to let go of this doubt, I am allowed to let it go.

Even though I don't know who I will be without this doubt, I will try to let it go.

Even though I am not sure if I want to let go of this doubt, I deserve to let it go.

Continue repeating the TAPPING ROUNDS, using your REMINDER PHRASES and RE-RATE your SUD's score.

My SUD's score: _____

Bringing in POSITIVE AFFIRMATIONS:
When your SUD's level is "2" or below, you can open-up, allowing more positive EMOTIONS into your life.
"If I didn't want to feel DOUBTFUL, what do I want to feel?"

CONFIDENT, REASSURED, OPEN, ACCEPTED, FREE, CHOICES

My REMINDER PHRASES:

EB - *I'm open to trying EFT-Tapping!*
SE - *I'm confident it will work for me*
UE - *I'm an adult now, I can choose to give it a try!*
UN - *I feel reassured that it can't hurt to try*
CH - *I'm allowed to let go of this doubt*
CB - *I deserve to be accepted*
UA - *I deserve to feel free*
ToH - *I'll give it a go*

Bringing in positive emotions too early is like spraying air freshener on your problem. It smells good, but it is still there! Work on your negative emotions behind your issue first.

REPEAT Steps 4 & 5 of the BASIC RECIPE, replacing your NEGATIVE EMOTIONS with your positive words as your REMINDER PHRASES, while doing TAPPING ROUNDS. Take a BREATH IN and OUT at the end of a few ROUNDS until your SUD's score is NEUTRAL or "0".

PALACE OF POSSIBILITY

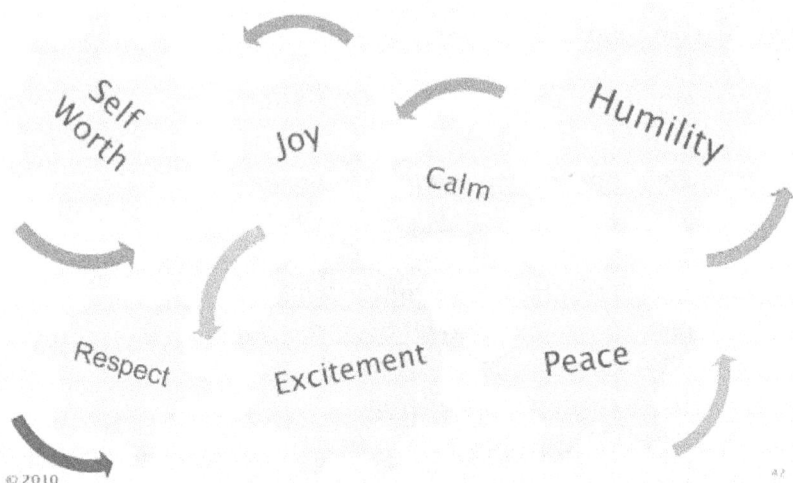

Self
Worth

Joy

Humility

Calm

Respect   Excitement   Peace

© 2010

Emotional Freedom Techniques
Every Feeling and Thought

**Open up your palace of possibility by writing a list
of negative emotions and choose one to tap on each day.**

SECTION 12
ASPECTS BEHIND YOUR STORY

In this section you will recognise that your STORY is like a book. It may be a short STORY, or your STORY may have many chapters, or ASPECTS, like a novel.

Your STORY can also be known as the TABLETOP, while the ASPECTS are the TABLE LEGS.

Your STORY or TABLETOP is quite general, for example - "DOUBT".

The TABLE LEGS are more specific. Some examples include:
"The time when I was 8 when I doubted that I could win the race".
"The time when I was 12 when mum doubted that I could make the right decision about what to wear to Grandma's party".
"The time when I was 16 and doubted if I would find a girlfriend".
"The time when I doubted if EFT-Tapping! would work for me".
"The time when my family thought what I was doing was stupid and doubted if Tapping would work for me".
"The time when I doubted if Sue, the author of this book, knew what she was talking about!"

Is your story a picture book, trilogy or epic drama?

You might notice during the investigation on DOUBT, that there are a few ASPECTS or TABLE LEGS to your PROBLEM. Each ASPECT can be INVESTIGATED individually. ASPECTS can include:

- Who was involved –
  Me
  Family members
  Sue the author

- What I heard / expressions used by my family –
  Why are you even trying this?
  It won't work for you.
  It's just the way you are. It's stupid!
  Condescending tone, scepticism in voice

- How I felt about myself and the expressions I used –
  Scared
  Silly
  Failure
  Doubtful – screwed up your nose while shaking head!

- What I thought to myself –
  Why am I doing this!
  I don't think it will work.
  What will my family say if I fail?
  Can I trust that Sue knows what she is talking about?

Other ASPECTS of your STORY can also include PHYSICAL FEELINGS like feeling sick in your tummy, this sinking feeling in your tummy; or fear such as failure. To further INVESTIGATE ASPECTS or TABLE LEGS of your PROBLEM you might like to pull up a recent event; or think of the first or the worse time that you can remember feeling "DOUBTFUL".

THE EMOTIONS BEHIND BULLYING BEHAVIOUR

⭐ Practise investigating one example of another ASPECT using one of the TABLE LEGS above or INVESTIGATE your own ASPECT.

That time when I felt (emotion): _____

➢ **WHO –**   Was involved: _____

➢ **SEE –**   Places/Room: _____

➢ **WHAT –**   Expressions did you notice: _____

➢ **HEAR –**   Sounds/Words: _____

➢ **WHAT –**   Tone of voice: _____

➢ **SMELLS –** Distinct odours if any: _____

➢ **TASTES –** Actual or perceived if any: _____

➢ **FEEL –**   Emotions experienced: _____

➢ **THINK –**   To self: _____

➢ **WHERE –**   Did you feel the emotions psychically: _____

➢ **HOW –**   Are you carrying these emotions:

Physically in your body – _____

Emotional well-being – _____

➢ **WHY –**   Are you holding on to these emotions or what are

you getting out of them by holding on to them:

_____

Remember that emotions and thoughts are different!
Overthinking the event causes paralysis by analysis!
You don't want an epic story – just state how you are feeling.

THE EMOTIONS BEHIND BULLYING BEHAVIOUR

⭐ If you are feeling confident you can continue to work on your ASPECT, or you might like to come back to this later.

1. IDENTIFY and NAME STORY – *The time when:* _____

_____

    My Problem: _____

    My Emotions: _____

2. SUBJECTIVE UNIT OF DISTRESS*:*

10 9 8 7 6 5 4 3 2 1 0

    My SUD's score: _____

3. SET-UP STATEMENT SEQUENCE:
   My SET-UP STATEMENT SEQUENCE x 3. TAP SIDE OF HAND.

    *Even though I feel*_____

    At _____

    For _____

    I deeply and completely accept myself;
    I will be OK; I choose to.......

THE EMOTIONS BEHIND BULLYING BEHAVIOUR

4. REMINDER PHRASES and TAPPING POINTS:

EYEBROW – _____

SIDE OF EYE – _____

UNDER EYE – _____

UNDER NOSE – _____

CHIN – _____

COLLARBONE – _____

UNDER ARM – _____

TOP of HEAD – _____

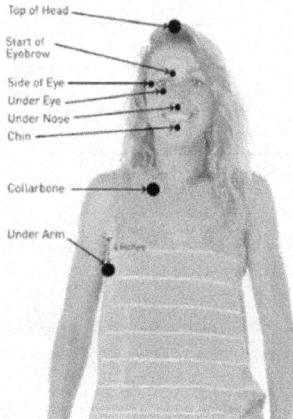

EFT images printed with permission from Dr Peta Stapleton

5. Take a BREATH IN and OUT. RE-RATE your SUD's score:

10 9 8 7 6 5 4 3 2 1 0

My SUD's score: _____

REPEAT STEPS 4 & 5 *of the BASIC RECIPE, take a BREATH IN and OUT. RE-RATE your SUBJECTIVE UNIT OF DISTRESS behind the DOUBT. Do you need to re-write one or more REMINDER PHRASES?*

    My SUD's score: _____

MY REMINDER PHRASES:

    EB - _____

    SE - _____

    UE - _____

    UN - _____

    CH - _____

    CB - _____

    UA - _____

    ToH - _____

Take a BREATH IN and OUT. RE-RATE your SUD's score

10　9　8　7　6　5　4　3　2　1　0

    My SUD's score: _____

REPEAT STEPS 4 & 5 of the BASIC RECIPE, take a BREATH IN and OUT. RE-RATE your SUBJECTIVE UNIT OF DISTRESS behind the DOUBT until you SUD's score has decreased further.

NEW SET-UP STATEMENT if stuck on low SUD's score:
Even though for whatever reason I'm stuck on a "3" and don't want to let go of this issue, I'm allowed to let it go.
Even though I don't know who I will be without this issue, I will try to let it go.
Even though I am not sure if I want to let go of this issue, I deserve to let it go.

Continue repeating the TAPPING ROUNDS, using your REMINDER PHRASES and RE-RATE your SUD's score.

My SUD's score: "2"

Bringing in POSITIVE AFFIRMATIONS:
"If I didn't want to feel (_____), how do I want to feel?"

(_____)

EB – *I'm_____*
SE – *I'm _____*
UE – *I'm an adult now, I can choose _____*
UN – *I am_____*
CH – *I'm allowed to let go of this _____*
CB – *I deserve to feel_____*
UA – *I deserve to be _____*
ToH – *I'm _____*

REPEAT STEPS 4 & 5 of the BASIC RECIPE, replacing your NEGATIVE EMOTIONS with your POSITIVE WORDS as your REMINDER PHRASES, while doing TAPPING ROUNDS. End with a BREATH IN and OUT and RE-RATE your SUD's until your score is NEUTRAL or "0".

★ SECTION 13
HOW BULLYING CAN FEEL TO YOU

In this section you will explore common EMOTIONS. Whether you are using bullying behaviour with others or you are being bullied, you are going to have some of these feelings. You can use EFT-Tapping! to deal with these umbrella emotions.

EVEN THOUGH I FEEL:

APATHY

GRIEF

FEAR

UNHEALTHY
DESIRE

ARROGANCE

UNWORTHY

ANGER

Apathy – giving up, drained, hopeless.

Grief – sad, heartache, helpless, nagging pain.

Fear – intimidated, scared, anxious, shy.

Unhealthy desire – impulsive, callous, manipulation, envy, controlling, power.

Arrogance - critical, judging, teaser, isolated, opinionated, patronising.

Unworthy – inadequate, pitiful, abandoned, ashamed, unloved.

Anger – mad, hostile, mean, guilty, depressed, temper, yelling, violent.

★ SECTION 14
BULLYING AT SCHOOL

Just like in your favourite spy show, you can INVESTIGATE what a bully might look like. At school, a bully tries to hurt, upset, take your things, laugh at or tease you, either while you are alone or when others are around to make themselves feel better or to look cool in front of others.

★ If you are being bullied, it may help to talk about what is happening, so you can work out a solution with a person in your support system:

1. When does bullying happen?

2. How does the bullying happen?

3. Where does the bullying happen?

4. Why do you think the bullying is happening?

Some of the answers to these questions could be when you are alone, when there is a group around, whenever the bully sees you. It could be that the bully knows what you hate or what you are afraid of and teases you about it. Bullying might happen in the classroom, playground, social media, at the park or shops.

Did you know that 90% of communication is non-verbal? This means that your actions, not your words, tell other people how you are feeling.

61

You give out different messages without even saying anything. A person's body language can send out signals to a bully, letting them know that you are confident, or if you are scared of them.

How can you improve your chances of not being bullied?

Relaxed — Head up, shoulders back, strong firm voice

CONFIDENT

Victim — Overwhelmed, fearful, angry, yelling, whining

REACTIVE

Target — *Shoulders rounded, eyes down, mumbles*

NOT CONFIDENT

Being bullied by others is not your fault. It has nothing to do with your looks, personality, race, or who you like. Bullying happens because the person doesn't know how to deal with their own problems, and they try to hurt others to make themselves feel better. This is why it can help if you look confident, are assertive and gain support from adults if you are feeling threatened by another person.

To have a strong voice, you need to express your point of view directly and firmly without yelling. It helps to use sentences that describe how you feel by starting with the word "I".

Be specific about how you are feeling.
"I feel upset when you tease me, stop teasing me now."
STOP!   STOP NOW!!

★ IDEAS TO TAP ON BEING BULLIED FOR KIDS.

Kids up to the age of 10 years only need to learn the SIDE OF HAND POINT or what can be explained to them as the Kid's FRIENDLY SPOT on their hand, and kids use 4 TAPPING POINTS on their face and upper body. Kids TAP with both hands on each side of the face and upper body TAPPING POINTS.

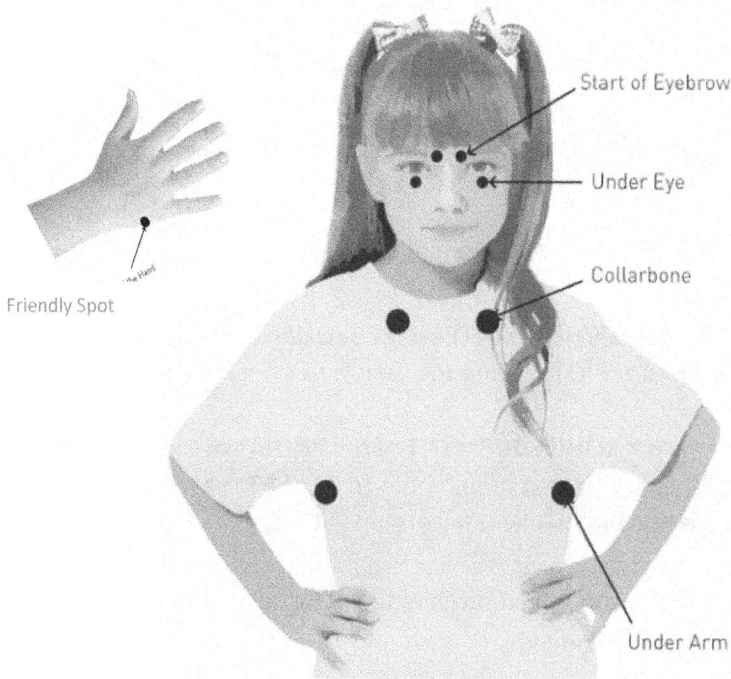

Start of Eyebrow
Under Eye
Collarbone
Friendly Spot
Under Arm

EFT images printed with permission from Dr Peta Stapleton

**Kids can tell you their whole problem for a
set-up statement in one sentence, if you listen to them.
"I feel_____, at_____, because_____."**

Kids can use their arms width to **CHECK** their **SUBJECTIVE UNIT OF DISTRESS (SUD's)** to show how big their **PROBLEM** is.

- If the child is 10, use the SUD's from 10 to 0.

- Wide arms for a huge PROBLEM, with the width decreasing to holding their hands together as they begin to calm down or clear away their PROBLEM.

What's for dinner?

- Kids may just change the subject when they are "over it"!

Kids use a **SET-UP STATEMENT SEQUENCE** while **TAPPING** on their **FRIENDLY SPOT,** saying the words aloud **x 3 times**.

Their **ACKNOWLEDGEMENT** of the **PROBLEM** can be any words that they relate to that helps them to **ACCEPT** that **EVEN THOUGH** they have this **PROBLEM**, they are an **OK** kid.

- Even though I am really sad at Katie for punching me, I am a good kid.
- Even though I hate her when she punches me, Mum and Dad still love me.
- Even though I feel like crying, I'm an awesome kid.

Kids **TAP** using both hands at once.

- **EYEBROW** - Using two fingers, pointer and middle fingers – like a magic wand, find the point at the inside of their eyebrow touching their nose, TAP 5 to 8 times.

- **UNDER EYE** - Follow the bone around to under the pupil, using pointer and middle fingers like a magic wand, TAP 5 to 8 times.

- **COLLARBONE** - Making a fist and gently thump the area under their collarbone 5 to 8 times – a bit like "Tarzan".

- **UNDER ARM** - Using the "flat" of their hand wrap their arms around their body and hug themselves while TAPPING 5 to 8 times. Alternatively, they can raise each elbow and TAP on the same side – a bit like a monkey scratching 5 to 8 times!

REMINDER PHRASES use the kid's EXACT words:
- Eyebrow -   I feel sad
- Under Eye -   I hate it when Katie punches me
- Collarbone -   It makes me so sad
- Under Arm -   I just want to cry

TAP just on the strongest emotion for a few rounds until you can see that their **SUD's** or arm **MEASUREMENT** has started to decrease.

After one or two **TAPPING ROUNDS, RE-CHECK** the **SUD's** or how sad they feel using the **MEASUREMENT** between their hands.

Repeat the **REMINDER PHRASES** and **RE-CHECKING** the **SUD's** until their hands are clasped together, or they are feeling OK, or they have forgotten what the **PROBLEM** was and have moved onto another conversation.

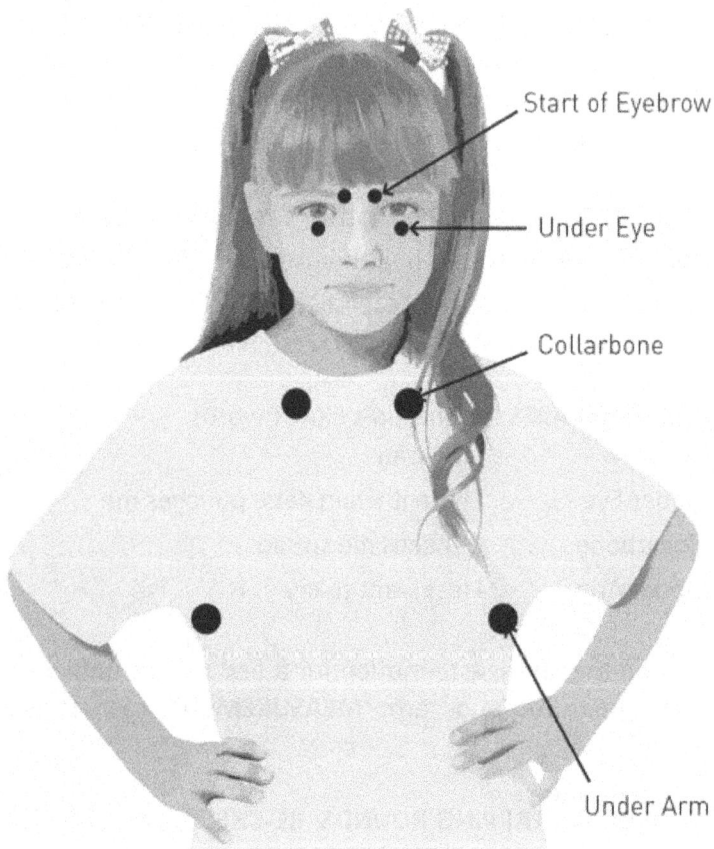

Start of Eyebrow

Under Eye

Collarbone

Under Arm

EFT images printed with permission from Dr Peta Stapleton

SECTION 15
ABOUT THE BULLY

WHY DO BULLIES ACT LIKE THIS?
Bullies do not know how to react positively to stress or PROBLEMS in their lives. They deal with their stress using inappropriate or unsafe ways of trying to control others as a form of coping. They may feel isolated and are looking for acceptance.

WHY DO PEOPLE BULLY OTHERS?
- Some people who bully persistently are likely to do so to dominate others and improve their social status;
- Some people have low self-esteem, show little regret for their bullying behaviour and do not see bullying as morally wrong;
- Some people may bully out of anger or frustration;
- Some people may struggle socially and could have also been victims of bullying.

THE FEELINGS BEHIND BULLYING BEHAVIOUR:
- Feeling guilty like it is your fault;
- Feeling hopeless/stuck like you can't get out of the situation;
- Feeling alone, like there is no-one to help you;
- Feeling like you don't fit in with the cool group;
- Feeling depressed and rejected by your family, friends, work colleagues and other groups of people;
- Feeling unsafe and afraid at home, school, work or within your community;
- Feeling confused and stressed out wondering what to do and why this is happening to you;
- Feeling ashamed that you are using bullying behaviour to control others or that the bullying is happening to you.

Here are some suggestions of bullying behaviours. Sometimes, you might do one or two of these things which are not so nice, but if you are doing a lot of these things to only certain people, on purpose to hurt them physically or make them upset, then you are acting like a bully or using bullying behaviours.

BULLYING BEHAVIOURS	✓ or X
1. Often use name calling, sarcasm or pick out faults	
2. Often have a defiant or hostile attitude to others	
3. Must have control of all situations	
4. Often rough – pushing, shoving, hitting, swearing	
5. Often involved in arguments or disagreements	
6. Don't care if I hurt other people's feelings	
7. Feel superior if I embarrass someone in public	
8. Force people to do things they don't want to	
9. Have a group who think what I do is cool	
10. People feel intimidated, scared, don't like me	
11. Pressure people into giving me their money/stuff	
12. Show aggression towards family, friends, adults	
13. Post inappropriate photos or comments	
14. Spread rumours about people or turn others against them	
15. Make jokes about race or someone's likes	
16. Feel important if people are failing as I look good	

Taken in part from: Bernados. s.d. *Bullying.* Accessed February 2019 at https://www.barnardos.ie/resources/young-people/bullying

Australian Human Rights Commission. *What is bullying?: Violence, Harassment and Bullying Fact sheet.* Accessed February 2019 at https://www.humanrights.gov.au/what-bullying-violence-harassment-and-bullying-fact-sheet

The bully is dealing with their own internal issues by using inappropriate or unsafe ways of handling their problems.

THE EMOTIONS BEHIND BULLYING BEHAVIOUR

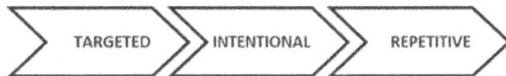

⭐ Ask yourself, "What am I getting out of bullying others?"

⭐ **TAPPING ON BULLYING BEHAVIOURS FOR KIDS.**

Bullying Behaviour = TARGETED INTENTIONAL REPETITIVE

SET-UP STATEMENT SEQUENCE:
Kid's FRIENDLY SPOT: Tap side of hand.
Tap x 3 times while saying:

Friendly Spot –
Side of Hand

- Even though I get mad and hit Jack, I'm still a good kid.
- Even though I yell at Jack, I try to be kind.
- Even though Jack never lets me play and I throw things, I'm an OK kid.

SUBJECTIVE UNIT OF DISTRESS SUD's:
- Kids over the age of 10 use SUD's score from 10 to 0.

10 9 8 7 6 5 4 3 2 1 0

I feel THIS MAD at JACK for NEVER LETTING ME PLAY.

TAPPING POINTS: Eyebrow; Under Eye; Collarbone; Under Arm

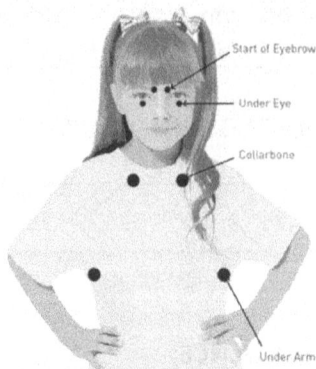

EFT images printed with permission from Dr Peta Stapleton

REMINDER PHRASES use the kid's EXACT words from what they have already told you while tapping on the each of the 4 tapping points 5-8 times:

I feel (emotion) MAD (at) JACK (for) NOT LETTING ME PLAY.

- I feel so mad (repeat a complete round using this emotion until SUD's decreases slightly)
- Eyebrow -   I yell at him
- Under Eye - I am mad at him
- Collarbone - I feel mad and hit him
- Under Arm - I get mad, and I throw things

After one or two ROUNDS, RE-CHECK the SUD's or how MAD they still are using the MEASUREMENT between their hands or SUD's score.

Repeat the REMINDER PHRASES and RE-CHECKING the SUD's until their hands are clasped together, or they are feeling OK, or they have forgotten what the PROBLEM was and have moved onto another conversation.

Can I go and play now?

You may have noticed in this scenario that perhaps the child doesn't have very good social skills and may not know how to play in a group setting. This child's way of getting the other children's attention might be by butting into the game, bossing them around or hitting them.

The child might not have good self-regulation or manage their emotions well, so they lash out, throw toys or become irritated and very angry quickly and take it out on other people.

Emotinal Freedom Techniques-Tapping! allows a child to say exactly how they are feeling, while the TAPPING part gives the child a safe way to deal with their feelings until they can calm down.

For a full demonstration of how to use EFT—Tapping with Kids, go to my Applied Techniques Training bonus tapping group: www.facebook.com/groups/bullyingbehaviour.

SECTION 16
ABOUT CYBERBULLYING

Unlike "the olden days" when bullying stopped at the school gate, today there is a growing issue on the effects of comments and posts left on social media. What this means is that bullying is now following a person into what may have been their place of protection, their home or bedroom.

The Australian Human Rights Commission states cyberbullying is bullying that is done using the Internet, a mobile phone, iPad, tablet or a camera to hurt or embarrass someone. It can be shared widely with a lot of people quickly and is difficult to remove once posted, which is why it is so dangerous and hurtful.

WHAT HAPPENS WITH CYBERBULLYING?

- A lot of people can view or take part in it;
- It is often done in secret with the bully hiding who they are by creating false profiles or names, or sending anonymous messages;
- It is difficult to remove a post from social media and can be duplicated to different places;
- It is hard for the person being bullied to escape if they use technology often;
- The content (photos, texts, videos) can be shared with a lot of people;
- This content may also be easy to find by searching on a web search site like Google.

WHAT DOES CYBERBULLYING LOOK LIKE?

- Being sent mean or hurtful text messages repeatedly;
- Receiving threats of physical harm to you or your family;
- Receiving dares to self-harm or kill yourself;
- Getting nasty, threatening or hurtful messages through social networking sites, or through sites where people comment online;
- Sending photos and videos of you to others to try and embarrass or hurt you;
- Spreading rumours about you via emails or social networking sites or text messages;
- Trying to stop you from communicating socially;
- Stealing your passwords or getting into your accounts and changing the information there;
- Setting up fake profiles pretending to be you or posting messages or status updates from your accounts.

STAYING SAFE WHILE USING SOCIAL MEDIA:

Phones or devices that connect to the internet are a privilege for children, not a right. As a parent or carer or family member, you need to protect your children by knowing who they are talking to online and be aware of when and where this is taking place.

This means having access to their passwords, only allowing the use of devices in common areas, specifying the time and place the device can be used e.g. not at the dinner table or in their bedroom and putting devices on charge outside of the bedroom at night.

OTHER WAYS OF PROTECTING YOURSELF FROM BULLIES ONLINE:

- Do not share your private information like passwords, name and address, phone numbers with people you don't know. This can also include sharing of photos of yourself, your friends and your family;
- Don't respond to messages when you are angry or hurt - either to strangers or people you know. This will often encourage them to continue or increase their harassment of you;
- Log out and stop messaging if you feel unsafe;
- Remember you have the option to block, delete and report anyone who is harassing you online and on your mobile;
- Find out how to report bullying and harassment on each of the different social networks that you use;
- Keep a record of calls, messages, posts and emails that may be hurtful or harmful to you;
- Remember to set up the privacy options on your social networking sites in a way you are comfortable with.

Taken in part from: Australian Human Rights Commission. 2011. *Cyberbullying: what is it and how to get help: Violence, Harassment and Bullying Fact sheet.* Accessed February 2019 at https://www.humanrights.gov.au/cyberbullying-what-it-and-how-get-help-violence-harassment-and-bullying-fact-sheet

Mobile phones and internet devices are a privilege, not the right of a child. Family rules are required around the use of social media.

WHAT DOES CYBER ABUSE LOOK LIKE?

Cyber abuse may also be known as behaviours including:

- Trolling;
- Flaming;
- Cyberbullying;
- Cyber hate;
- Cyber violence;
- Cyber mobbing;
- Cyber stalking;
- Cyber harassment;
- Cyber racism and online hate speech;
- Technology-facilitated abuse;
- Sextortion;
- Image-based abuse.

Like other types of bullying, these behaviours need to show larger or serious patterns of targeted online abuse, and therefore likely to have a seriously threatening, intimidating, harassing or humiliating effect on a person. Some comments that may not be considered bullying or abuse include:

- Sarcastic comments;
- Insults;
- Strong opposing views;
- Off-topic statements that deliberately derail conversation threads.

THE EMOTIONS BEHIND BULLYING BEHAVIOUR

The Office of the eSafety Commissioner provides information on reporting incidences of cyberbullying for children and teens under the age of 18 years.

1. Contact the social media service to report the incident;
2. Collect evidence through URLs or web addresses, screenshots, scanned printouts of any messages or photos and videos;
3. Make a report to the Office of the eSafety Commissioner.

The Office of the eSafety Commissioner will work with you to have cyberbullying material removed from any service.

https://www.esafety.gov.au/complaints-and-reporting/cyberbullying-complaints

Some of the emotions behind how a person may feel around the issue of cyberbullying can include:

- Feeling of guilt that it is their fault;
- Hopeless or stuck in the situation;
- Isolation and being alone;
- Fear of not fitting in;
- Feeling depressed and angry;
- Rejection by others;
- Feeling unsafe and afraid;
- Feeling confused and stressed out about why this is happening or how to stop it;
- Ashamed that it is happening to them, or that other people will believe what is being said.

Cyberbullying is the most cowardly form of bullying. The bully is hiding behind a screen making hurtful comments to people who they may not even know to make themselves feel better or look cool. Often this allows a bully to make comments that they wouldn't have the guts to say to someone face to face.

If there are enough of the same comments or a large number of "shares" or "likes", the person being cyberbullied may begin to believe that what is being said is true. This may tear apart the last piece of this person's self-worth leading to depression, self-harm, suicidal thoughts or suicidal attempts.

★ **IDEAS FOR TAPPING ON BEING CYBERBULLIED.**
Children up to 10 years can use the following instructions. Teens and Tweens can follow the BASIC RECIPE from Section 4.

SET-UP STATEMENT SEQUENCE:

Friendly Spot –
Side of Hand

Kid's FRIENDLY SPOT: side of hand.
Tap x 3 times while saying:

- Even though I get hurt by what is said online, I'm still a good kid
- Even though I'm scared that others will hate me, my family loves me
- Even though I don't know how to make them stop, I am safe

78

SUBJECTIVE UNIT OF DISTRESS (SUD's):

- Kids over 10 years use a SUD's score from 10 to 0.

10 9 8 7 6 5 4 3 2 1 0

I feel THIS HURT by JANE for SAYING THINGS ABOUT ME.

TAPPING POINTS: Eyebrow; Under Eye; Collarbone; Under Arm

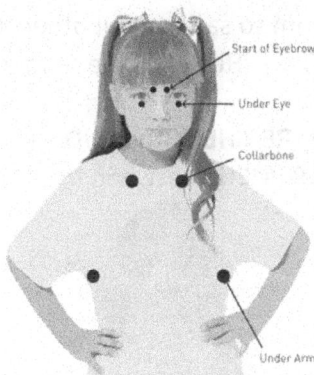

Start of Eyebrow
Under Eye
Collarbone
Under Arm

EFT images printed with permission from Dr Peta Stapleton

THE EMOTIONS BEHIND BULLYING BEHAVIOUR

REMINDER PHRASES use the kid's EXACT words from what they have already told you. Do a complete round using one emotion OR a reminder phrase on each point. You can do one or more rounds. Some examples may include:

I feel (emotion) HURT (by) PEOPLE (for) SAYING THINGS ONLINE ABOUT ME THAT AREN'T TRUE.

- Eyebrow -   I feel SO HURT (when they tease me)
- Under Eye -   I feel so isolated (when they are mean)
- Collarbone - I feel so alone (when they pick on me)
- Under Arm - I am scared (that they will never stop)

- Eyebrow -   Everyone hates me
- Under Eye -   I just want them to stop
- Collarbone - I feel scared because I can't stop them
- Under Arm - I don't feel safe, no-one wants me around

- Eyebrow -   I don't know why they are doing this to me
- Under Eye -   Maybe they are right, I am just hopeless
- Collarbone - I am so sad, what if others believe them
- Under Arm - This is HURTING me so much

After a few **ROUNDS, RE-CHECK** the **SUD's** or how **HURT** they still are using the **MEASUREMENT** between their hands or **SUD's** score.

Repeat the **REMINDER PHRASES** and **RE-CHECKING** the **SUD's** until their hands are clasped together, or they are feeling OK, or they have forgotten what the **PROBLEM** was and have moved onto another conversation.

Once you see that the child is becoming considerably calmer, include some **POSITIVE AFFIRMATIONS** about things that they do well, or things they or other people like about them. These affirmations can also be used in the **SET-UP STATEMENT.**

- I have people who love and support me
- I am safe with my family and friends
- I deserve to have a good life
- I am a super awesome kid
- I have friends who like me
- I am a friendly person
- I deserve to be happy
- I know what is true
- I am a kind person
- I am just right
- I am loveable
- I am wanted
- I am healthy
- I am loving
- I am smart
- I am funny
- I am safe
- I am free
- I am...

I'm safe and loved

SECTION 17
BULLYING IN A RELATIONSHIP

BULLYING WITHIN THE FAMILY UNIT involves constant name-calling and put-downs, intimidation, guilt, blame, shame, physical aggression or threats, taking or breaking items and psychological mind games. This bullying can take place between two adults, an adult and a child, a child and an adult, or two or more siblings.

If you think the bullying behaviour is a warning sign that you may be in a domestic violence situation, please seek professional help.

Bullying in a family is not bickering or a disagreement or difference of opinion. It is a repeated, intentional, targeted physical, verbal or psychological aggression towards a vulnerable family member who doesn't have the skills to protect themselves from a person with real or perceived difference in power. The bullying actions can be seen to be trying to take control of a family member's property or to hurt them physically or emotionally. The family member being bullied may feel helpless and ashamed. They become stressed and may withdraw, living in an environment where they don't feel safe and accepted.

The bully or bullying behaviour may be hard to identify. The bully may appear to be "nice" to the family member in public but may taunt the family member when no-one else is around. Victims of bullying within a family are often hurt and confused. Home should be a safe place but for some people this is not the case. The bullies within a family are skilled at picking out vulnerabilities and manipulating fears and insecurities.

THE EMOTIONS BEHIND BULLYING BEHAVIOUR

Bullies within the family may feel threatened by other family members and become highly competitive over-achievers. Perhaps they show a low level of empathy, gaining pleasure out of seeing others hurt or in pain; or they lack a sense of self-worth.

Bullying between adult partners may be motivated by a difference of power and a desire to improve one's status and control over a peer. This can be seen as intimidation, put-downs, or by how conflict is handled in a relationship. For a relationship to be strong, there are two statements you should never use: "You always" or "You never".

For more information on how to create a healthy relationship, see
The Secret to Winning Relationships – www.winningrelationships.net

BULLYING BETWEEN ADULT CARERS and CHILDREN has a fine line between bullying and a carer's perception of discipline. Discipline should be firm but non-threatening. Ideally, consequences for an action should be pre-arranged so that the child understands what is expected, what is accepted and what the outcome will be. This consequence should be reasonable and should be followed through without on-going guilt or blame of the child. Discipline that is harsh, belittling and intimidating may actually be bullying.

Physical aggression is not a form of discipline. Aggression causes anxiety and uncertainty and teaches the child that using aggression is an acceptable form of conflict resolution. If this action is repeated by a parent or carer, it could be perceived as bullying behaviour.

If a child has a social or emotional disorder, you cannot discipline a symptom of the disorder. The child can't help being impulsive or anxious. You can look at the behaviour behind the disorder and deal with the behaviour in a fair and just manner, while respecting the child as a person.

For more information, check out SIMPLY ADHD/ASD www.appliedtechniques.net

Not being actively involved in a child's life or showing favouritism for one child over another child may encourage bullying behaviours between siblings as they "fight" for your love and attention.

BULLYING BETWEEN CHILDREN and ADULT CARERS may be manipulation tactics that a child uses to take control over a situation or change the adult carer's mind.

Children use badgering, intimidation, threats, buttering-up, whinging or physical actions as a way of getting what they want. Children only use these tactics if they are working for them.

★ Think about a favourite tactic your child uses.
What are they getting out of it?

SIMPLY 1-2-3® Parent Management program delivered by Applied Techniques Training uses the teachings of Dr T. W. Phelan's original 123 Magic.

BULLYING BETWEEN SIBLINGS When it comes to bullying, there doesn't seem to be any differences between the sex of the child, age or placement in the family. It is thought that boys are more likely to bully younger siblings, while girls are more likely to bully an older sibling. Bullying seems to take place between siblings who are closer in age.

Sibling rivalry can be seen as a form of bullying.

A study undertaken in 2007 states that domestic violence (bullying) between siblings is more prevalent than domestic partner abuse or child abuse or even schoolyard bullying.

Emma O'Friel. 2018. *Sibling bullying: humiliated and scorned by a family member . . . this is not just 'sibling rivalry'*. Accessed February 2019 at https://www.irishtimes.com/life-and-style/health-family/sibling-bullying-humiliated-and-scorned-by-a-family-member-this-is-not-just-sibling-rivalry-1.3327426

Negative behaviours that sometimes look like sibling rivalry may be thought of as abuse or bullying. In an article published in the Journal of Family Violence 2016, most parents/carers thought of abuse as "just" sibling rivalry as:

- Normal;
- Not serious;
- The victim's fault;
- A private matter;
- Taboo.

This attitude to sibling rivalry tells the bully that their behaviour is acceptable and lessens the support of the child who is being bullied.

LONG-TERM RISKS OF BULLYING FOR THE VICTIM:
- Chronic depression;
- Withdrawal;
- Self-harm;
- Increased risk of suicidal thoughts, suicide plans/attempts;
- Anxiety disorders;
- Post-traumatic stress disorder;
- Poor general health;
- Self-destructive behaviour, including self-harm;
- Substance abuse;
- Difficulty establishing trusting relationships.

LONG TERM EFFECTS OF BULLYING FOR THE BULLY:
- Risk of becoming a spousal or child abuser;
- Risk of antisocial behaviour;
- Substance abuse;
- Less likely to be educated or employed.

★ **IDEAS FOR TAPPING ON BULLYING WITHIN RELATIONSHIPS.**

For EFT-Tapping! your STORY of "BULLYING" is like the TABLETOP. You need to INVESTIGATE ASPECTS or TABLE LEGS behind your STORY. A relationship can be within a family, friends, teachers, coaches, work mates, community members.

INVESTIGATION: *That time when (my partner called me a totally stupid bitch in front of the family, AGAIN, for "ruining" the roast):*

➢ **WHO –** Was involved: *me, my partner, mum, my sister*
➢ **SEE –** Places/Room: *at home in the kitchen*
➢ **WHAT –** Expressions did you notice: *eye rolling*
➢ **HEAR –** Sounds/Words: *you ruin everything, hopeless*
➢ **WHAT –** Tone of voice: *exaggerated*
➢ **SMELLS –** Distinct odours if any: *rum*
➢ **TASTES –** Actual or perceived if any:
➢ **FEEL –** Emotions experienced: *not appreciated, can't do anything right.*
➢ **THINK –** To self: *I am doing the best I can; it's only a roast; give me a break; I do everything around here; nothing is ever good enough; maybe he is right.*
➢ **WHERE –** Did you feel the emotions: *heart*

THE EMOTIONS BEHIND BULLYING BEHAVIOUR

> **HOW –**   Carrying these emotions:
        Physically in your body – *tight chest; heartbroken*
        Emotional well-being – *low self-esteem, self-doubt*
> **WHY –**   Are you holding on to these emotions or what are
        you getting out of them by holding on to them:
        Security, protection – where would I go?

1. IDENTIFY and NAME your STORY:
    The time when – *I didn't feel appreciated by my partner.*
    My Problem: *Always being put down no matter what I do*
    My Emotions: *hurt, afraid, helpless, worn out, on edge.*

2. SUBJECTIVE UNIT OF DISTRESS:

10 9 8 7 6 5 4 3 2 1 0

    My SUD's score: *"8"*

3. SET-UP STATEMENT SEQUENCE:
    What is the strongest emotion I am feeling?
    Who is the person, or self, associated with this feeling?
    What happened to me to feel this way?

My SET-UP STATEMENT SEQUENCE.
TAP SIDE OF HAND while saying the following three times:
    Even though I feel *unloved,*
    At *home by my partner,*
    For *picking on everything I do*

    I deeply and completely accept myself;
    I will be OK; I choose to accept I am a capable person.

4. REMINDER PHRASES and TAPPING POINTS:
The words you use come from your investigation!

EYEBROW -	*These put-downs*
SIDE OF EYE -	*Feeling unloved by my partner*
UNDER EYE -	*Doubt if I will ever be good enough*
UNDER NOSE -	*Embarrassed in front of my family*
CHIN -	*Feeling unappreciated*
COLLARBONE -	*Never get anything right*
UNDER ARM -	*Feeling worn out by the put downs*
TOP of HEAD -	*Tired of having to live on the edge*

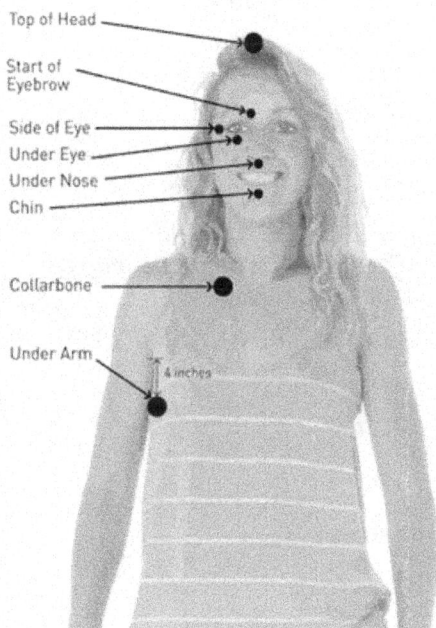

EFT images printed with permission from Dr Peta Stapleton

5. Take a BREATH IN and OUT. RE-RATE your SUD's score:

10 9 8 7 6 5 4 3 2 1 0

My SUD's score: "5"

REPEAT STEPS 4 & 5 of the BASIC RECIPE, take a BREATH IN and OUT, RE-RATING your SUBJECTIVE UNIT OF DISTRESS behind the hurt you feel from your partner.

My REMINDER PHRASES:

EB -	*Feeling unloved*
SE -	*I'm not good enough*
UE -	*I'm afraid to be alone*
UN -	*How dare he talk to me like this*
CH -	*I doubt if anyone could love me*
CB -	*I'm walking on a knife's edge*
UA -	*I feel helpless, I can't take it anymore*
ToH -	*Feeling unloved by my partner*

Take a BREATH IN and OUT. RE-RATE your SUD's.

10 9 8 7 6 5 4 3 2 1 0

My SUD's score: "3"

NEW SET-UP STATEMENT if stuck on low SUD's score:

> *Even though for whatever reason, I don't want to let go of this issue, I am allowed to let it go.*
> *Even though I don't know who I will be without this issue, I will try to let it go.*
> *Even though I am scared to let go of this issue, I deserve to let it go.*

Continue repeating the TAPPING ROUNDS, using your REMINDER PHRASES and RE-RATE your SUD's score.

> *My SUD's score: "2"*

Bringing in POSITIVE AFFIRMATIONS:
"If I didn't want to feel unloved, how do I want to feel?"

(Loved, Safe, Appreciated, Respected, Happy, Free, Calm)

- **EB –** *I'm safe;*
- **SE –** *I am loving and lovable to others;*
- **UE –** *I'm an adult now, I choose to feel respected;*
- **UN –** *I am allowed to be happy and calm;*
- **CH –** *I'm allowed to let go of this feeling of hurt;*
- **CB –** *I deserve to feel appreciated;*
- **UA –** *I deserve to be happy and safe;*
- **ToH –** *I am free to love myself just the way I am.*

REPEAT STEPS 4 & 5 of the BASIC RECIPE replacing your NEGATIVE EMOTIONS with your POSITIVE WORDS as your REMINDER PHRASES while doing TAPPING ROUNDS with a BREATH IN and OUT until your SUD's score is NEUTRAL or "0".

Use EFT-Tapping! to break the cycle!

SECTION 18
BULLYING IN THE WORKPLACE

WORKPLACE BULLYING is not about conflict between two equally powered parties. It is not about being transferred, demoted, disciplined, counselled in your work role or being dismissed from your place of employment. Although it may seem unfair to you, it is not bullying if it is done in a transparent, reasonable, respectful and fair manner.

When it comes to bullying, the health, well-being and integrity of the target has been comprised. Bullying is a systematic, target-focused campaign by a person on the interpersonal well-being of an industry peer, co-worker or junior member of the workplace.

The perpetrator may be threatened by the competence, strengths, emotional intelligence or likability of the target, or they may be unreasonably pressured or "bullied" themselves from a higher level to provide outcomes and "meet the bottom line".

Bullying can include verbal, physical, social and psychological abuse, some of which are criminal offences.

THE AUSTRALIAN HUMAN RIGHTS COMMISSION tells us that bullying can have other implications within the law:

BULLYING OF A MINOR is lawfully seen as child abuse if the target is under 16 years old.

BULLYING IS DISCRIMINATION if it is because of your age, sex, pregnancy, race, disability, sexual orientation, religion or specific other reasons. Sexual harassment and racial hatred are also against the law.

BULLYING IN THE WORKPLACE could happen to anyone in the workplace: managers, employees, apprentices, interns or students. It may be a paid or non-paid employment as a casual, part-time or permanent worker.

The actions of bullying behaviours in a workplace may come from a single manager, supervisor, employee or colleague, or a group of people in the workplace. The perpetrator may use their influence to isolate the target so that co-workers no longer stand up for the target. The bully may be secretive about their actions so that others don't notice.

The bully may be out to destroy the target's standing in the workplace, jeopardising relationships, physical and mental health, and the career of the target.

If you are being bullied, it's important that you know there are things you can do and people who can help. You have the right to be in a safe workplace free from violence and harassment.

**Bullying is a health, work and safety hazard;
it is not a form of active management.**

THE AUSTRALIAN HUMAN RIGHTS COMMISSION tells us bullying in the workplace is:

- Repeated hurtful remarks or attacks, or making fun of your work or you as a person including your family, sex, sexuality, gender identity, race or culture, education or economic background;
- Sexual harassment, particularly stuff like unwelcome touching and sexually explicit comments and requests that make you uncomfortable;
- Excluding you or stopping you from working with people or taking part in activities that relate to your work;
- Playing mind games, ganging up on you, or other types of psychological harassment;
- Intimidation that is making you feel less important and undervalued;
- Giving you pointless tasks that have nothing to do the job;
- Giving you impossible tasks that can't be done in the given time or with the resources provided;
- Deliberately changing your work hours or schedule to make it difficult for you;
- Deliberately holding back information you need for getting your work done properly;
- Pushing, shoving, tripping, grabbing you in the workplace;
- Attacking or threatening with equipment, knives, guns, clubs or any other type of object that can be used as a weapon;
- Initiation or hazing – where you are made to do humiliating or inappropriate things to be accepted as part of the team.

IF YOU ARE BEING BULLIED AT WORK, you might:

- Be less confident in your work;
- Be less active or successful;
- Feel scared, stressed, anxious or depressed;
- Have your life outside of work affected, e.g. study, relationships;
- Want to stay away from work;
- Feel like you can't trust your employer or the people whom you work with;
- Lack confidence and happiness about yourself;
- Have physical signs of stress like headaches, backaches, sleep problems.

The irony of bullying is that the perpetrator and the target may be having the same feelings, but one is expressing these feelings externally, while the other is holding on to these feelings internally.

EMPLOYERS have a legal responsibility under Occupational Health and Safety and Anti-discrimination laws to provide a safe workplace. Employers have a duty of care for your health and well-being while at work. An employer that allows bullying to occur in the workplace is not meeting this responsibility.

The solution is to make both the perpetrator and the target healthier, physically and emotionally using EFT-Tapping!

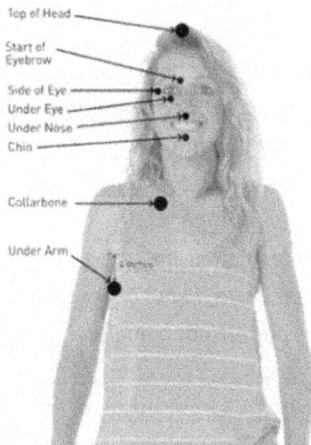

EFT images printed with permission from Dr Peta Stapleton

THE FIVE BASIC INGREDIENTS:

1. Investigate your **PROBLEM.**
2. Guess your **SUBJECTIVE UNIT OF DISTRESS – SUD's** score.
3. Create a **SET-UP STATEMENT** by **TAPPING** the **SIDE OF HAND** while **REPEATING THE STATEMENT** aloud x **3.**
4. **TAP** on each of the 8 individual **TAPPING POINTS** while saying your **REMINDER PHRASE** to complete a **ROUND.**
5. Take a **BREATH IN and OUT. Re-rate your SUD's score.**

★ IDEAS FOR TAPPING ON BULLYING IN THE WORKPLACE.

For EFT-Tapping! your STORY of "BULLYING" at the office is like the TABLETOP. You need to INVESTIGATE ASPECTS or TABLE LEGS behind your STORY.

INVESTIGATION: *That time when (my line manager put me down, yelling at me during a staff meeting for making a mistake in the data spreadsheet):*

- ➤ **WHO –** Was involved: *me, manager, other staff*
- ➤ **SEE –** Places/Room: *boardroom, manager hovering*
- ➤ **WHAT –** Expressions did you notice: *scorned*
- ➤ **HEAR –** Sounds/Words: *how stupid, you know better*
- ➤ **WHAT –** Tone of voice: *snarling*
- ➤ **SMELLS –** Distinct odours if any: *stale cigarette smoke*
- ➤ **TASTES –** Actual or perceived if any: *bitter taste*
- ➤ **FEEL –** Emotions experienced: *humiliated, embarrassed, angry, put down, not respected/ accepted/valued as part of the team*
- ➤ **THINK –** To self: *it was an honest mistake, how dare you speak to me like that, my colleagues think I am hopeless at my job, I'm going to lose my job, she has unreasonable expectations that I should just know what to do*
- ➤ **WHERE –** Did you feel the emotions: *chest, head*
- ➤ **HOW –** Carrying these emotions:
  Physically in your body – *sore knee, headaches*
  Emotional well-being – *anxiety, fear, "stuck"*
- ➤ **WHY –** Are you holding on to these emotions or what are you getting out of them by holding on to them:
  Survival – need the job even if it is "doing my head in".
  If I let go, she will win.

THE EMOTIONS BEHIND BULLYING BEHAVIOUR

1. IDENTIFY and NAME YOUR STORY:
   The time when – I didn't feel valued as a staff member in my company by my boss
   My Problem: Regularly yelled at by my boss
   My Emotions: angry, fearful, anxious

2. SUBJECTIVE UNIT OF DISTRESS:

   10 9 8 7 6 5 4 3 2 1 0

   My SUD's score: "8"

3. SET-UP STATEMENT SEQUENCE:
   What is the strongest emotion I am feeling?
   Who is the person, or self, associated with this feeling?
   What happened to me to feel this way?

My SET-UP STATEMENT SEQUENCE.
TAP SIDE OF HAND while saying the following three times:

   Even though I feel humiliated,
   At work by my line manager,
   For yelling at me in front of other staff members

   I deeply and completely accept myself;
   I will be OK; I choose to accept I am a smart person

4. REMINDER PHRASES and TAPPING POINTS:
The words you use come from your investigation!

EYEBROW – *This bullying behaviour*

SIDE OF EYE – *Feeling bullied by my line manager*

UNDER EYE – *Feel anxious when I am yelled at*

UNDER NOSE – *Embarrassed in front of my colleagues*

CHIN – *Feeling bullied at work*

COLLARBONE – *Bullied by my boss*

UNDER ARM – *Feeling humiliated for making a mistake*

TOP of HEAD – *This bullying behaviour by my boss*

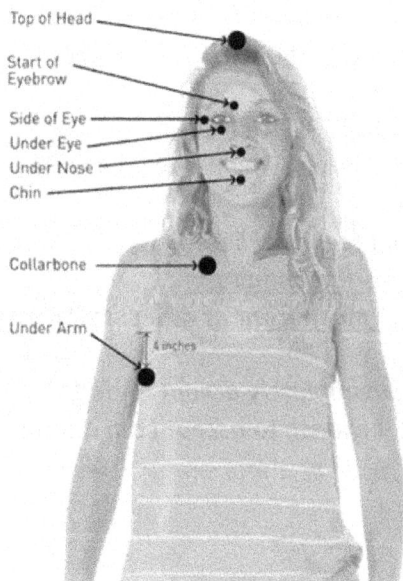

EFT images printed with permission from Dr Peta Stapleton

5. Take a BREATH IN and OUT. RE-RATE your SUD's score:

10 9 8 7 6 5 4 3 2 1 0

My SUD's score: "5"

REPEAT STEPS 4 & 5 of the BASIC RECIPE, take a BREATH IN and OUT, RE-RATING your SUBJECTIVE UNIT OF DISTRESS behind the humiliation you feel about by your boss in front of other staff members.

My REMINDER PHRASES:

    EB -   **Feeling humiliated**
    SE -   **I'm feeling stuck, can't move forward**
    UE -   **I need the job to survive**
    UN -   **How dare she treat me like this**
    CH -   **The staff will think I can't do my job**
    CB -   **This is "doing my head in"**
    UA -   **I feel helpless**
    ToH -   **Feeling bullied by my boss**

Take a BREATH IN and OUT. RE-RATE your SUD's.

10 9 8 7 6 5 4 3 2 1 0

My SUD's score: "3"

NEW SET-UP STATEMENT if stuck on low SUD's score:

> *Even though for whatever reason, I don't want to let go of this issue, I am allowed to let it go.*
> *Even though I don't know who I will be without this issue, I will try to let it go.*
> *Even though I am not sure if I want to let go of this issue, I deserve to let it go.*

Continue repeating the TAPPING ROUNDS, using your REMINDER PHRASES and RE-RATE your SUD's score.

> *My SUD's score: "2"*

Bringing in POSITIVE AFFIRMATIONS:
"If I didn't want to feel humiliated, how do I want to feel?"

(Acknowledged, Accepted, Valued, Respected, Confident)

> EB – *I'm safe;*
> SE – *I have a lot to offer;*
> UE – *I'm an adult now, I choose to feel confident;*
> UN – *I am a capable, successful person;*
> CH – *I'm allowed to let go of this feeling;*
> CB – *I deserve to feel valued;*
> UA – *I deserve to be appreciated;*
> ToH – *I'm respected within the workplace.*

REPEAT STEPS 4 & 5 of the BASIC RECIPE replacing your NEGATIVE EMOTIONS with your new POSITIVE WORDS as your REMINDER PHRASES while doing TAPPING ROUNDS with a BREATH IN and OUT until your SUD's score is NEUTRAL or "0".

Bullying in the workplace can cause on-going stress related problems which end up costing the company time and money.

★ TAPPING ON OTHER ASPECTS.

As part of the investigation above, you may notice some PHYSICAL ASPECTS of the PROBLEM. The investigation identified heart palpitations and headaches. When TAPPING on PAIN in EFT-Tapping! it is essential to define the pain, working on the worse pain first following the BASIC RECIPE.

★ IDEAS FOR TAPPING ON PHYSICAL PAIN.

1. NAME your PAIN: *This pain in my* _____

- ➢ **WHEN –** Did it start? Do you feel this pain the most?

- ➢ **WHERE –** Where is the pain in your body? Does it move?

- ➢ **SEE –** What shape is this pain?

- ➢ **FEEL –** What texture is this pain?

- ➢ **HEAR –** If this pain was a noise, what would it sound like?

- ➢ **SMELL –** What smell does this pain remind you of?

- ➢ **TASTE –** What taste would you describe this pain as?

- ➢ **THINK –** If this pain was a colour, what would it be?

- ➢ **WHO –** Who or what does this pain remind you of? Why?

- ➢ **WHAT –** If there is an emotional reason, what would it be?

- ➢ **HOW –** How much does this pain weigh?

- ➢ **WHY –** Why are you holding on to this pain?

THE EMOTIONS BEHIND BULLYING BEHAVIOUR

2. SUBJECTIVE UNIT OF DISTRESS – PAIN LEVEL

10 9 8 7 6 5 4 3 2 1 0

My SUD's score: _____

3. My SET-UP STATEMENT SEQUENCE
TAP SIDE OF HAND while saying the following three times:

Even though I have this pain in my_____,

I deeply and completely accept myself;
I will be OK; I choose to...

4. REMINDER PHRASES and TAPPING POINTS

EYE BROW –   *(type) _____*
SIDE OF EYE –   *(when started) _____*
UNDER EYE –   *(emotion) _____*
UNDER NOSE – *(shape/texture/colour) _____*
CHIN –   *(hear/smell/taste/noise) _____*
COLLARBONE – *(who remind of/why) _____*
UNDER ARM – *(weight) _____*
TOP of HEAD – *(what are you getting out of holding it)*

_____

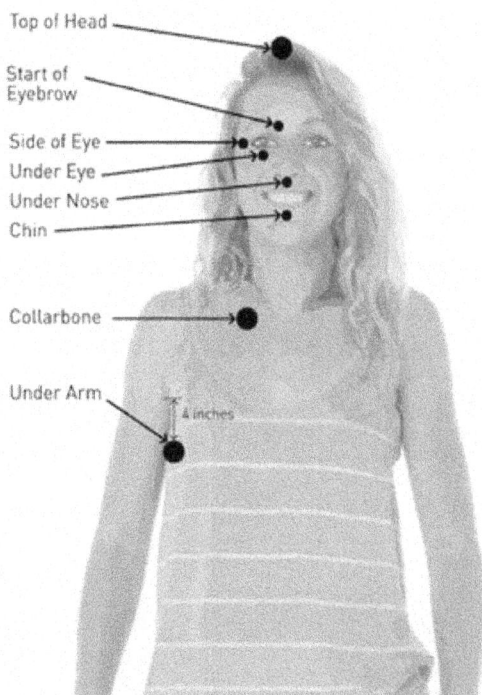

EFT images printed with permission from Dr Peta Stapleton

5. Take a BREATH IN and OUT. RE-RATE your SUD's score:

My SUD's score: _____

REPEAT STEPS 4 & 5 of the BASIC RECIPE, take a BREATH IN and OUT, RE-RATING your SUBJECTIVE UNIT OF DISTRESS behind the PAIN until your SUD's score is NEUTRAL or "0".

SECTION 19
TAPPING OUT BULLYING

Society suggests that we need to change the culture in the home, schoolyard or workplace. I have not known a time in our society when it has been acceptable to hurt someone deliberately or to stand by and watch someone being hurt by others either physically or emotionally. Bullying behaviour is not a culture, it is discrimination.

You will have learnt by now that there are many people hurt as a result of every bullying incident. A BYSTANDER is someone who sees or knows about bullying that is happening to someone else. A BYSTANDER might be a partner or family member, friend, teacher, classmate, coach, an employer, manager, supervisor or colleague.

BYSTANDERS can either be part of the bullying problem or an important part of the solution to stop bullying. BYSTANDERS are hurt by both sides of bullying behaviours.

Don't turn your back on bullying.

THE EMOTIONS BEHIND BULLYING BEHAVIOUR

BYSTANDERS can act in different ways when they see or know about bullying:

1. Some bystanders take the side of the bully by laughing at the target, encouraging the bully, or by passing on text messages or posts on social media sites;
2. Some bystanders will give silent approval or encourage the bully by looking on;
3. Some bystanders may watch or know about the bullying but don't do anything. They may not know what to do or are scared. This group of bystanders knows that bullying is not ok;
4. Some bystanders will be supportive and take safe action to stop the bully, find help or support the target.

There is no one-size-fits-all approach to being a supportive BYSTANDER. For supportive bystanders to take safe and effective action here are some suggestions:

- Make it clear to your friends that you won't be involved in bullying behaviour;
- Never stand by and watch or encourage bullying behaviour;
- Do not harass, tease or spread gossip about others, this includes on social networking sites like Instagram;
- Never forward on or respond to messages or photos that may be offensive or upsetting;
- Support the person who is being bullied to ask for help e.g. go with them to a place they can get help or provide them with information about where to go for help;
- Report it to someone in authority or someone you trust e.g. at school to a teacher, or a school counsellor; at work to a

manager; if the bullying is serious, report it to the police; if the bullying occurs on Facebook, report it to Facebook.

Australian Human Rights Commission. 2011. *What you can do to stop bullies - Be a supportive bystander: Violence, Harassment and Bullying Fact sheet.* Accessed February 2019 at https://www.humanrights.gov.au/what-you-can-do-stop-bullies-be-supportive-bystander-violence-harassment-and-bullying-fact-sheet

BYSTANDERS have a moral responsibility to help create a positive, safe environment. Don't enable bullying behaviour by joining in or ignoring the bullying behaviour. If someone you know is experiencing bullying, it is important to keep yourself safe and to accept that you may not be able to change the bully, but you can provide both parties with information from:
https://www.humanrights.gov.au or https://www.esafety.gov.au

A bully will only change if they want to. You can't change someone else's bullying behaviour. You can change the way you react to the behaviour by using Emotional Freedom Techniques-Tapping! to investigate the emotions behind the behaviour and tap into your self-worth.

⭐ **IDEAS ON TAPPING FOR BYSTANDERS**

1. The STORY I want to work on today is:
   The time when _my 10-year-old daughter, Jess, was picked on at school and I felt guilty and helpless._

2. The SUD's score for this PROBLEM is: _"8"_

3. The SET-UP STATEMENT SEQUENCE I'm going to say 3 times while tapping on the SIDE OF HAND/KARATE CHOP point is:
   Even though I feel _(Emotion) guilty because (Person) Jess was (Reason) picked on for being overweight_

   I deeply and completely accept myself / I am doing my best / I'm an OK mum.

4. The REMINDER PHRASES I am going to use to TAP each POINT:
EB -	**_I feel so guilty_**
SE -	**_I couldn't protect Jess_**
UN -	**_It is my fault Jess is overweight_**
CH -	**_Jess didn't deserve it_**
CB -	**_I feel like no-one supported us_**
UA -	**_I am doing the best I can_**
ToH -	**_I feel helpless_**

5. Take a BREATH IN and OUT. SUD's score:
   ROUND 1: _7_ ROUND 2: _5_ ROUND 3: _2_ ROUND 4: ___

POSITIVE AFFIRMATION:
I am doing the best I can to show Jess love and support.
I am good enough; It's not my fault; Jane needs help.

Different feelings, people, pains - ASPECTS that came up:
When I was bullied at work and didn't stand up for myself.

SECTION 20
YOUR FINAL ANSWER

As a final resolution, you may like to say what you need to say to another person involved in your problem. Although it may not be safe to do this directly to the person, it is safe to say what you need to say or need to hear in your mind.

★ Below is an exercise that you can use as a final resolution:

- Place your thumb on one side of your collarbone point and your four fingers on the other side. Hold your fingers on this point firmly and still and breath evenly in and out;
- Close your eyes;
- In your mind, picture the person you have the issue with;
- See their face, notice their posture, hear their voice;
- Imagine what you need to tell them about how you felt;
- Imagine hearing what you need them to say to you (not what they would normally say or have said in the past but what you would like them to say to you);
- Once you have expressed your feelings and have heard what you need from them, you can: walk side by side as peers; if the person has passed away you can carry them on your shoulder to watch over you; or if the person is someone that you no longer want in your life, turn away and confidently walk in the opposite direction.
- When you are ready, gently remove your fingers from your collarbone point, open your eyes, take a breath in and out and come back to the here and now, noticing things around you, and note how calm and relaxed you are now feeling.

THE EMOTIONS BEHIND BULLYING BEHAVIOUR

MY EFT-TAPPING! IDEAS @Applied Techniques Training 2010

1. The STORY I want to work on today is: ***The time when***

_____

2. The SUD's score for this PROBLEM is: _____

3. The SET-UP STATEMENT SEQUENCE I'm going to say 3 times while tapping on the SIDE OF HAND/KARATE CHOP point is:

Even though I have this (Emotion) _____
(Person) _____ ***(Reason)*** _____

_____
I deeply and completely accept myself.

4. The REMINDER PHRASES I am going to use to TAP each POINT:
EB – _____
SE – _____
UN – _____
CH – _____
CB – _____
UA – _____
ToH – _____

5. The SUD's scores for following ROUNDS are:
ROUND 1: _____ ***ROUND 2:*** _____ ***ROUND 3:*** _____ ***ROUND 4:*** _____
and other ROUNDS: _____

POSITIVE AFFIRMATION: _____

Different feelings, people, pains - ASPECTS that came up:

_____

THE EMOTIONS BEHIND BULLYING BEHAVIOUR

MY EFT-TAPPING! IDEAS FOR PHYSICAL PAIN.

1. NAME your PAIN: *This pain in my* _____

- ➤ **WHEN** – When did it start? Do you feel this pain the most?

- ➤ **WHERE** – Where is the pain in your body? Does it move?

- ➤ **SEE** – What shape is this pain?

- ➤ **FEEL** – What texture is this pain?

- ➤ **HEAR** – If this pain was a noise, what would it sound like?

- ➤ **SMELL** – What smell does this pain remind you of?

- ➤ **TASTE** – What taste would you describe this pain as?

- ➤ **THINK** – If this pain was a colour, what would it be?

- ➤ **WHO** – Who or what does this pain remind you of? Why?

- ➤ **WHAT** – If there is an emotional reason, what would it be?

- ➤ **HOW** – How much does this pain weigh?

- ➤ **WHY** – Why are you holding on to this pain?

ABOUT THE AUTHOR:

Sue Suchocki was born in Brisbane, Australia, and grew up with her mother and father, Monica and Bill Townsend, along with her 3 siblings and extended family members. Sue's dad passed away when she was 13 years old while her mum lived to the age of 92. Sue worked in cartography where she met and married her husband, Victor, in 1985. Sue and Victor have two adult children and one granddaughter.

Sue was involved in advocating for family members who were vulnerable due to intellectual, emotional and social impairments. Sue has worked for Education Queensland and the Department of Communities – Child Safety and has been an active volunteer and advocate within her local community.

In 2008, Sue was introduced to Emotional Freedom Techniques by her now friend and colleague Pamela O'Leary from Guided Solutions. Sue gained a Certificate IV in Training and Assessment and has since completed parts I to IV as a student of Gary Craig, FasterEFT – Robert Smith, and is a certified Clinical EFT Universe practitioner. Sue remains current in the field of EFT through research and master classes delivered by Dr Peta Stapleton PhD – Evidence Based EFT.

In 2010, Sue's goal of opening a training organisation was reached with the registration of Applied Techniques Training®. Applied Techniques Training now delivers workshops, including *ADHD/ASD – The Game Plan*; *SIMPLY ADHD/ASD*; *SIMPLY 1-2-3*; *Surviving Your Adolescents*; *Managing Angry Adolescents Differently* and *Managing the Bull* to individuals, parents, carers, educators, health professionals and community service staff, students and volunteers.

Sue's dream was to share the techniques she has learned through personal and professional experiences with others to apply in their situation. Sue is achieving this dream as the author of this, her first book in the "The Emotions Behind" series, using her knowledge of EMOTIONAL FREEDOM TECHNIQUES-TAPPING! and experience in behaviour strategies as a speaker and presenter.
Sue Suchocki – Emotionologist - Applied Techniques Training
www.appliedtechiques.net
Facebook – facebook.com/appliedtechniquestraining
Bonus Tapping Group – facebook.com/groups/bullyingbehaviour/

GLOSSARY

Acupressure Points – Specific points on the body that are stimulated, often through massage, to relieve pain.

Applied Techniques Training – www.appliedtechiques.net

Aspects – More specific information about the event or thoughts behind the event that came up as a general problem e.g. The time when….

Breath In and Out – At the end of each tapping round, take a deep breath in and out. A relaxing way to end a round is to clasp your wrist gently with the other hand while taking this breath.

Bully – Person who often hurts or frightens other people.

Bullying – The repeated use of threats or violence in an attempt to harm or intimidate another.

Cognitive Empathy – Recognition and understanding of another's emotional state.

Crying or Extreme Distress – Keep tapping without using any words while keeping your eyes open until you feel calmer and can continue with your story.

Cyberbullying – The use of electronic communication to bully a person, typically by sending messages of an intimidating or threatening nature.

Doubt – A feeling of uncertainty or lack of conviction.

Emotion – A feeling behind a situation that you are in or the people you are with.

Emotional Intelligence – awareness of one's own emotions and moods and those of others, especially in managing people.

THE EMOTIONS BEHIND BULLYING BEHAVIOUR

Emotions behind the problem – How you felt about the event.

Emotions under the umbrella – Apathy, Grief, Fear, Unhealthy Desire, Arrogance, Unworthiness, Anger.

Emotional Freedom Techniques – EFT, Tapping or EFT-Tapping!, is a self-regulation tool that can provide stress relief for physical, emotional, and performance issues.

Emotional Freedom Techniques Discovery Statement – "The cause of all negative emotions is a disruption in the body's energy system". Gary Craig.

EFT Basic Recipe –
Investigate your problem;
Guess the rating of your Subjective Unit of Distress (SUD's) with 10 being intense and 0 being neutral;
Create a set-up statement sequence to say 3 times while tapping on your hand;
Create reminder phrases to say while tapping a round;
Breath in and out;
Re-rate your Subjective Unit of Distress.

Energy Systems – Energy that flows through your body along defined pathways, such as your meridians.

Event – Something of significance to you that happened in the past.

Exposure Therapy – Being safely exposed to a phobia or fear.

For results that are TERRIFIC, be SPECIFIC!

Hand Measurement – The width between your hands (arm width) that can be used to rate your subjective unit of distress.

Gentle Tapping – If crying or overly distressed, use only the name of your story in your set-up statement sequence while saying only the words, "this story" as your reminder phrases until you have a SUD's of below 5 or you are comfortable to use the words from your investigation.

Issue – An event that happened in the past that caused negative emotions, distress or physical pain.

Karate Chop or Side of Hand point – Used by tapping this point while saying SET-UP STATEMENT SEQUENCE to complete a sequence to identify and accept the problem.

Kids checking and re-checking – How bad their problem is.

Kids Friendly Point – Name for side of hand point used by kids.

Kids Tapping Points – Start of eyebrow, under eye, collarbone, under arm.

Kids Tapping Instructions – Use both hands; two fingers for eyebrow and under eye; make a fist and gently thump for collarbone; flat hand wrapped around their body like hugging themselves while tapping with a flat hand.

Measuring Intensity – Subjective unit of distress (SUD's) or using arms width to show how "big" the problem is.

Name Your Story – The title you give to an event that reminds you of what happened but doesn't cause you a high SUD's intensity.

Negative Emotions – Uncomfortable feelings you have about your past or things that happened to you.

Neutral Feeling – The feeling you have when your problem / emotion has decreased to a "0" or it isn't bothering you anymore.

New Set-Up Statement – Is only required if you get stuck on a SUD's number, e.g. 4 or lower. Even though for whatever reason I can't let go of this emotion I am allowed to let it go; even though I don't know who I will be without this problem, I will try to let it go; even though I am not sure if I want to let go of the problem, I deserve to let it go.

Palace of Possibility – Write a list of negative emotions and investigate when they have occurred during your life. Tap on one issue a day until you work through them all.

Perpetrator – The person who carries out harmful acts, e.g. the bully.

Positive Affirmations – Introduced once SUD's score is 2 or less using positive words. If you don't want to feel (this negative emotion), how do you want to feel (positive emotions)? Replace your reminder phrases with these positive affirmations.

Problem – An event that happened in the past that causes you concern or distress.

Problem Investigation –Who was involved; see where you were; what expressions did you notice; what did you hear/words/tones/smells; what emotions did you feel; what did you think; where did you feel the emotions in your body; how are you carrying these emotions physically/emotionally; why are you holding on to these emotions.

Psychological Reversal – Blockages within your thoughts that are stopping your progress in solving a problem.

Physical Aspects – Pain, sick feelings, heart flutters, aches, headaches, stiff or sore joints.

Reminder Phrases – A short phrase relating to your emotions taken from investigating your problem. The reminder phrases are said while tapping on each individual tapping point.

Re-rate SUD's – After saying your reminder phrases while tapping each point, breath in and out. Re-rate your SUD's score until neutral.

Resilience – The ability to bounce back or recover quickly from an uncomfortable situation.

Secondary Gain – A benefit you may get from holding on to negative emotions e.g. protection, a feeling of "winning".

Set-Up Statement –
Even though I have this (emotion)
at (person)
for (reason)
I deeply and completely accept myself; I am an OK person;
I choose to be_____.

Set-Up Statement Sequence – Using the set-up statement wording while tapping on the side of hand point.

Set-Up Statement Number of Times – The set-up statement is repeated 3 times while continuously tapping side of hand.

Set-Up Statement Purpose – Acknowledges the problem, the related emotions and accepts it.

Set-Up Statement Questions –
What is the strongest emotion I am feeling?
Who is the person or yourself, associated with this feeling?
What happened for me to feel this way?

Side of Hand or Karate Chop Point – Used by tapping this point while saying set-up statement to complete a sequence to identify and accept the problem.

Somatic Therapy – The relationship between the mind and the body.

Sore Spot – A spot near the Collar Bone area which can be rubbed in a circular motion as an alternative to the Karate Chop point or Side of Hand point. Please note it is not the Collar Bone tapping point.

THE EMOTIONS BEHIND BULLYING BEHAVIOUR

Story – Remembering and acknowledging the negative emotions behind your story while accepting yourself as a good person anyway.

Subjective Unit of Distress / SUD's score – Guess the rating of the intensity of your emotions at this time. 10 = really intense; 8 = intense; 6 = annoying; 4 = slightly annoying; 2 = irritating; 0 = neutral.

Sympathetic Nervous System – Activates what is often referred to as your fight or flight response.

Tabletop – A general statement of the problem e.g. I am feeling anxious; I am angry.

Table Legs – An aspect of the problem which is more specific e.g. The time when...

Tapping Points – Side of Hand, Eyebrow, Side of Eye, Under Eye, Under Nose, Chin, Collarbone, Under Arm, Top of Head.

Tapping Pressure – Firm enough to feel it, soft enough not to hurt.

Tapping Instructions – Pointer and middle fingers for eyebrow, side of eye, under eye, under nose, chin; All fingers and thumb or fist for collarbone; 4 fingers or flat of hand for under arm; all fingers and thumb for top of head.

Tapping Number of Times – 5 to 8 times on each tapping point to complete a round.

Tapping Round – While saying the reminder phrases, tapping 5 to 8 times on each tapping point. Breath in and out and relax (this may be done while gently clasping your wrist with your other hand).

Target – The person who is being harmed by the acts of other people e.g. being bullied.

NOTES: _____

_____

_____

_____

_____

_____

_____

_____

_____

_____

_____

_____

_____

_____

_____

_____

_____

_____

_____